ALMOST INTERESTING

ALMOST INTERESTING

THE MEMOIR

DAVID SPADE

DEY ST.

AN IMPRINT OF WILLIAM MORROW *PUBLISHERS*

DEY ST.

A hardcover edition of this book was published in 2015 by Dey Street Books, an imprint of William Morrow Publishers.

FIRST DEY STREET BOOKS PAPERBACK EDITION PUBLISHED 2016.

Designed by Suet Chong

Library of Congress Cataloging-in-Publication Data has been applied for.

ISBN 978-0-06-237699-2

19 20   OV/LSC   10 9 8 7 6 5 4 3 2

To my lovely mom, the real writer in the family and the strongest person I know (excluding Arnold Schwarzenegger). Bryan, Andy, and I would be nowhere without you. Thanks for not bailing when things got tough. Tough being an understatement.

CONTENTS

INTRODUCTION		ix
ONE	GROWING UP	1
TWO	MAMA'S BOY	13
THREE	LOSING MY VIRGINITY	19
FOUR	MINI SPADE	27
FIVE	JOINING A FRATERNITY	37
SIX	GETTING SOME HEAT	49
SEVEN	LOSING MY HEAT	61
EIGHT	HBO *YOUNG COMEDIANS SPECIAL*	79
NINE	GETTING ON *SNL*	87
TEN	*SNL* 1990–1991	99
ELEVEN	*SNL* 1991–1992	117
TWELVE	*SNL* 1992–1993	129
THIRTEEN	*SNL* 1993–1994	139
	BEING VALUABLE	149
FOURTEEN	EDDIE MURPHY AND ME	153
FIFTEEN	*TOMMY BOY*	161
	A FEW MORE THINGS ABOUT CHRIS	175
SIXTEEN	SKIPPY	179
SEVENTEEN	MY FIRST HOOKER	187

EIGHTEEN   MY HOUSEKEEPER   191
NINETEEN   A VICTORIA'S SECRET PARTY   199
TWENTY   CHICK TRICKS   209

EPILOGUE   THE TIME I DID TOO MUCH
                  COKE   221
ACKNOWLEDGMENTS   227

INTRODUCTION

Hey. Welcome to my stupid book. I wrote it myself, so I'll take all the blame. I had so many titles when I decided to do this. My friend said it's like having a kid, naming it is the best part, and then the rest is shitty. Kidding! But the rest of writing it is actually hard work, which is not my strong suit. I had a few title pitches that were considered in my first meeting then promptly shot down day one after I signed up. I thought *My Stupid Life* wasn't bad and we could run with that. But that was shot down. Then I tried *My Life as a 10*. I liked that. Sort of funny. (Because I'm only a 9.) I liked *Dear Diary* because it was nice and vague. Then came *Rags to Bitches*. That was briefly discussed, but bookstores said no. And of course *Punchlines and Pussy* never made it out of the gate. So we landed on the one you see now. I'm good with it.

FYI, this book is not that serious. This is meant to be read when super bored, then forgotten fifteen minutes later. It could be read cover-to-cover during one medium-to-severe case of diarrhea. Nothing in it will change your life. There are no easy tips to lose belly fat like I see on my computer every day. It's just me blabbing away about my life and *SNL* and getting beat up by my assistant and any other stupid shit I could think of. It's easy to read, no big words cuz I don't know any. It's like watching *Dolphin Tale* on

HBO and then forgetting you ever saw it. By the way, I did see *Dolphin Tale* and didn't forget it. In fact I had a few problems with it . . . this might not be the forum for this, but quickly: It's about a dolphin with a bad attitude who gets caught in some lobster traps and his tail gets chopped off and so he's fucked. He's basically an anchor because he doesn't have a rudder. He starts freaking out so people start to help him and for some reason he's a dick about it. They make him a crummy little tail out of popsicle sticks or whatever and he doesn't like it. This is where I'd say "It's for your own good, dipshit!" but he's not having it. Then they get a doctor to make a better one and he's still being a pussy. He smashes it against the wall and breaks it. Like, "I hate it! It's not my real tail! I hate the ocean! I hate everyone!!!" Full Jan Brady tantrum. Then he realizes it helped and starts nudging the fake tail like, "Put it back on, I get it now," and they are like, "Fuck off, you don't want it, remember?? You're so fucking tough! Have fun drowning, moron, because this is going on a shark now. You're an asshole."

Anyway, I feel I went off on a tangent, but I think what I'm saying is my book is like *Dolphin Tale* but with fewer jokes.

Have a nice read!

CHAPTER ONE
GROWING UP

I was supposed to die. That's what seven different doctors in a row told my parents. I came out a month early, a superpreemie (I think that is the street term). I was probably about five pounds and roughly the size of a hacky sack or a medium-size gerbil. To make matters worse, I couldn't eat anything without barfing it all up. I was allergic to everything, so I couldn't put on weight. It was all very scary to the parental units (warning: *Coneheads* reference). All I could choke down was goat's milk, of all things. So gross. The hardest part was taking that goat everywhere. (JOKE NUMBER ONE, FOLKS! Stay close: there are four more buried in this book somewhere.) Thank God Mom and Dad kept hammering away at different doctors because eventually, they found one who said, "I've seen this shit before. (Very casual doctor.) When he's a year old he will grow out of it and start eating regular food." The dude was right; when I turned a year old I climbed out from under that goat and said, "Fuck this, let's go to Wendy's!" Obviously I have bulked up to my present athletic appearance since then, but it was touch-and-go there for a while. You can all relax. Spade is ripped and ready for the Combine (NFL reference).

By the way, my parents met when Dad was in the air force as a radar man (the biggest pussy job) and Mom was a sweet, attractive little debutante who went from private schools to Denison University in Ohio. They both attended and I guess the sparks flew. I can't imagine the sparks but they tell me they were there. So in a major playa move my dad, Sammy, put a ring on it and my mom was looking forward to a very quiet, normal life in the Midwest raising a family with her doting husband nearby. (We will find out how this plan went off the tracks later. These "hooks" keep you reading!)

Needless to say, growing up I was pretty microscopic, and I hated it. I wasn't just short, I was "Oh fuck I hope everything's cool with this kid. Maybe he's actually a hamster" short. I'm one of three kids. All dudes. Bryan, Andy, and David. B.A.D., as my mom joked. (She's not a pro comedian so I didn't expect an LOL out of that.) I'm the baby. And compared to my brothers I looked like a baby, and I acted like a baby, too. I was such a gigantic pussy/ mama's boy growing up it was almost comical. Actually, not almost comical. It is comical. Now. At the time, it was just plain sad. Anyone could beat me up, at any time. I was fragile. And I was always scared.

I'll back up a bit. I was born in Michigan. (Fuck this book—it's boring already. Pick up the pace, Spade.) When I was four, my dad had the great idea to move from Michigan (where he was from and where my brothers and I were all born) to Arizona. I think the move was motivated by my dad's desire to cheat on my mom in a different state. Apparently he had plowed through Michigan (literally) and was ready to take on the valley of the sun. Sammy wasn't super reliable, so once we got there it became clear that he didn't have the job he said he did, so he grabbed some temp sales job at a magazine that didn't pay jack shit. Then he scrammed on the family and that was that. No calls, no alimony, no child support. Crickets across the board. So my mom, who is truly a saint, had the unfortunate job of raising three selfish rug rats, with little to no income in a town she didn't know with zero friends around. The least Dad could have done was bail out on her in Michigan so she had some peeps around, but he was too selfish to be that thoughtful.

So here we were frying in the desert with no dough, and no plan. My Mom had to go out and get two jobs. However, this was the seventies, when guys were assholes and women didn't get paid anything. (It's sort of like today! Yay, progress!) So she worked constantly, as a secretary and also doing sales at a department store, while my brothers and I were constantly bitching about not having enough of everything. (Why don't I have a surfboard?! etc.) It must have been tough on her. Mom would break down sometimes, but mostly she wouldn't complain and tried to make her ungrateful children happy. My dad would show up once a year and give me a Nerf football for Christmas and act like he was my hero. (Oh my God it's two colors—you spoil us!) You prick. The thing was, he *was* sort of a hero when he came around. When your dad isn't there, you wonder what the fuck you did to make it so bad to make him go. It's not like his kids were accidents. He'd planned to have a family. Then he couldn't take the presh and skadoodled, leaving Mom with zero babysitting money and skimpy food rations. So when he came to visit, it was like the pope had come to town or something; we were all over him. So embarrassing. Not really fair to Mom, but that's just the way it works when you are a kid.

She'd sit there leaning, in her robe, against the curtains, smokin' her Slims going, "He's a real hero."

You know, I never really noticed I was poor. When you're a kid, you just find shit to do around the house or yard to keep yourself busy. If you've never had badass toys, you don't really miss them. And people around us were poor, too, so I fit right in. I had no complaints. I used my imagination to entertain myself. I also had a rock collection and a beer can collection I was very proud of. These were my mom's ideas. I didn't realize till later this was genius on her part. "Hey Davey, you should collect rocks and cans! THEY'RE FREE! While you're at it, collect old cigarettes butts and broken glass too." It was very crafty of her. I'm not bragging, but I had mica, pyrite, and an amethyst in my collection oh yea. (Side note to historians: Amethysts, those big purple crystal ones, were a big panty dropper back in the day. Even the big old-school seventies panties, with the louvers on 'em.) Dinners at home usually consisted of the five main food groups: tater tots, fish sticks, mac and cheese, Oreos, and cereal. Some combination of these. With a Coke or milk. She did her best; later we moved up to Lean Cuisine. We were ballin'. It was a real Lil' Wayne time for us.

From day one, I was the school pipsqueak. In class pictures they sat us shortest to tallest and I was always first. It was me then girl, girl, girl, girl, girl, girl, girl, then the next guy. To be shorter than every chick was so humiliating, and made me the ultimate bully bait. In third grade a fellow student came up to me during recess and said, "Hey Spade, I heard your family's poor." Being in the dark about this fact, I was like, "What? Oooohhh, yea, no, you got some bad information." A few hotties from my class were drifting by, and they stopped to listen. By the way, being poor isn't the real panty dropper you think it is, even in third grade. Chicks were like "Let him answer . . . !" The guy said again, "I hear you guys have no money." I was like nervous, I was thinking, *What a dick! Why are you cock-blocking me?! Dude I don't even know you!* So I tried to defend myself. I said, in a sort of "I rest my case" tone, "Would we have *two* tires on our front yard if we were poor?" He was like, "Uhhh, yeah?" So I keep going: "Would I be wearing the same thing every day if I was poor?" Now this one didn't sound good as it came out. And then, it all sort of hit me. We were broke. And that sucked. But my mom was sneaky. She'd say, "That outfit looks so good on you, why don't you wear it tomorrow?" Classic bamboozle. That day was the end of my poverty innocence. You'd think at some point my dopey brothers might have tipped me off.

In addition to being the shortest and now the poorest, I also had the worst school supplies. My crayons were always that little ghetto four-pack my mom swiped from IHOP and stuffed in her bra ("nothing for me today, thanks"). These came with the four basic colors: blue, red, green, yellow. One day this foxy chick, who should have been in pre-supermodel school instead of my dogshit class, was sitting next to me said, "Hey, can I borrow a crayon?" I was like, BOOOIOIOIOIOIOINGGG! Wiener went up so fast it did a gainer. This brat had never talked to me and now we have some chatter going. I couldn't fumble it. This is not a drill! All these thoughts were going through my head. But I played it cool. "Why sure . . ." as I looked through my four nubby little crayons, trying to pick one that wasn't broken. Then she coyly upped the ante: "Do you happen to have Burnt Sienna?" I froze. In my head, I was thinking, *WTF? How 'bout red you little grub worm?* But I didn't freak out. I still was playing my Fonzie attitude. "Um, let me check . . ." (Mumbling as I sifted through them.) "Hmm . . . yellow . . . blue . . . yellow again . . ." I was stalling.

Then out of nowhere some rich prick in back of me chimed in: "I have Burnt Sienna." I turn around and saw that he had the mega-box of sixty-four Crayolas. Like a cinder block. Biggest one you can get. It even has a balcony. Every goddamn color in the rainbow was in there, so many they are squirting out the sides. It even had Clear! Who needs Clear? It does nothing! It's like writing with a booger. So he plucked it out and without warning started sharpening it on the back of the box! There was a sharpener on the back! It was so cool. A hush fell over the room. Even I was freaking out. All the chicks were staring in disbelief. They were so turned on. I'm serious, there was not a dry pussy in the place. Even the teacher was drenched . . . it was like Splashdown! Kaaaatrina! Niiiiiagra! He handed the crayon to her and she slid off her chair in ecstasy. Of course, she never looked at me again. So you can see, I've always had a way with the gals. This proved I needed some game.

When I was about nine my mom married a doctor. He was a very tall, very bald, very eccentric guy named Howard P. Hyde, and the polar opposite of my real dad, Sammy. This guy was *no* fun, had *no* personality, *did* have a job, *was* responsible, *and* gave a fuck about us. My mom liked the change of pace. Not sure she was ever in love with him because he was a bit quirky and not exactly *GQ* material, but he wanted to save us and apparently he was okay with Judy being only 5 percent into him. He was a little strange, but I liked him. He was from South Dakota. I'd never known anyone from there before and haven't since. I never called him Dad, but I came close once. It just felt too weird. Even so, I almost kicked over and used his last name, Hyde. Spade Sr. hadn't given me any reason to be proud of my heritage or anything. But when some kid I was riding bikes with said to me, "Hey Hyde, lets go hit 7-Eleven!" I realized that doesn't sound as cool as "Spade." Howie did have some lasting influences on my life. He introduced me to coin collecting, chess, and guns. (Wow, Spade, you were a total nerd.) Chess, you say? Well, this may come as a shocker but I was a smart kid. Hyde liked that because he was a member of Mensa and had gone to Duke. (Talk about a major nerd alert when he whipped out that Mensa card . . . sirens went off.) So, we bonded over smarty-pants things. He convinced me to take German in high school because he was fluent.

I really can't think of a more useless language or waste of my high school time than taking a semester of German, especially since we lived in Casa Grande, Arizona. This is a dumpy copper mining town two hundred miles from THE MEXICAN BORDER! PEOPLE! HOW 'BOUT I TAKE SPANISH? SOMETHING I MIGHT FUCKING USE EVERY DAY OF MY LIFE! But no, German it was. So I struggled through an elective and now I can maybe hit on Heidi Klum one day. (*Guten Tag, Heidi! Hast du einen Bruder? Nein aber ich habe zwei Schwestern!* Translation: "Do you have any brothers? No, but I have three sisters." Yeah baby! That was right out of the German 101 textbook and, shockingly, never came in handy.)

So Howie was a smart guy, but mostly he was a little nuts. For instance, he gave me a shotgun and a shotgun shell reloader for Christmas. When I was TEN, FOLKS. I was like, "Well, I wanted a skateboard, but that's cool?" So now it's sixth grade, I've got some street cred because peeps found out I had a shotgun. I went skeet shooting with Howie and reloaded all my own shells. I played chess, even making it to the state chess finals before I had to drop out. I got whomped with German measles in a cruel turn and I was laid out for twelve days. What a bummer. I almost croaked; BTW actually that's the closest I've come I think. I also read the most books in my school (forty-seven in one year) *and* was spelling bee champ. (I got smoked in the first round at state though. How could I choke on *apparatus*? I was like A-P-A . . . Wait! No A-P-P . . . GONG!!) I was king of the local nerds with my nerdy stepdad. All was good. So I thought.

Then, my stepdad started getting a little crazier and crazier. He had been a doctor during the Vietnam War, so he had post-traumatic stress syndrome. Not that we knew that then. We just thought he was being a weirdo cause that's what you called it then. He would have flashbacks of battles and wake us up in the middle of the night to go out looking for the enemy, wearing his green army helmet and carrying a gun. A live, loaded gun. We would play along. Why not? Seemed like fun to three boys, until one night when he accidentally blew a hole in the roof of his closet. That's when it got a bit "quirky-heavy" for me.

My brothers and I were three little white trash troublemakers running around our shitty mining town blowing up bullfrogs and horny toads with M-80 firecrackers, freezing locusts and tying dental floss around them so when they unfroze we could fly them around like locust kites, and causing all sorts of *Joe Dirt*–style trouble. My oldest brother, Bryan, was the craziest of our gang. He had a cage in his room filled with five rattlesnakes. He also had a boa constrictor and a python. And I thought nothing of it. *Umm, WTF??* That's a lot of reptile in one house. Who were we? Marilyn Manson? Once we tried to add to Bryan's collection by catching a rattler that was chillin' in our front yard. We were trying to catch it with two tennis rackets. The idea was to grab the snake behind the head by pinching the rackets together and then push it into an empty plastic milk jug (white trash 101). Well, Howard Pierre Hyde pulled up, drunk as yoozsh. (This was when cops didn't hassle you for driving drunk. Aka the good old days.) The man drank a case of Coors tallboys every day, so that wasn't so unusual. He saw what we were up to and yelled out, "Why are you pussyfooting around? You just pick it up." He grabbed the snake with his bare hands. (I always knew there was a reason why you don't just pick up snakes. They BITE.) And naturally, it bit him. He didn't even flinch. He just said, "Well, I'm going to go take a nap." My brothers and I looked at each like, "No shit dude, I bet you will." Howie took off his shirt and flopped on the couch, and we just stood and stared at him. In twenty minutes his whole side swelled up and turned purple and we watched it happen live (shout-out to Andy Cohen). We shook him awake and called an ambulance. He was in pretty rough shape for a while there but eventually pulled through. We still kept all the snakes in the house, though. We learned zero from that.

My stepdad also had a buddy from the army who lived near us with his family. This dude had married a Vietnamese girl during the war which was common and she already had four kids when they got hitched. Howard P. Hyde helped the family come to the States, and they actually lived IN OUR HOUSE for a while. Um, let me do the math for a second. Their family of six. Our family of five. That's a grand total of eleven assholes in that shit shack. As you can imagine, that didn't last too long, so they skedaddled over to the trailer park (shout-out to Kid Rock!). Then we had to go over to the trailer park and hang out with these kids. Their names were, in order, Shin, Que, Trang, and Lan. Not exactly Manny, Moe, and Jack. They were close to our ages, probably like eight, seven, six, and four. I have to say, I barely remember these kids at all, I remember Trang being kind of hot. I'm not super into Asians like all my friends, but Trang drew some plasma down to my dick region. Always sporting a slutty barrette, barely knowing English. It all worked for me. I was too young to know about sex, but I knew I was digging her and things were getting a little tingly in wiener town. Her mom must have caught on because she never let me hang out with her. Shin and I hung out the most. He was around my age and he was the smartest one of that crew, so we had a lot to bond over just telling each other we were smart. That year, Shin and I were even put ahead in school two grades for reading and math. (That's right, folks, you didn't hear me wrong, *two* grades, not one!) I'd be talking to the ladies in my third-grade class going, "Oh shit, look at the time. Hey gals, gotta scoot. I got to trot down the hall to fifth grade for reading and math. We're doing a little thing called fractions, yawn, you wouldn't understand. No big. Don't wait up . . ." pretty solid rap for a third grader, if I do say so.

We had a pretty good run with old Howard, all in all. The sad part came when I was about fifteen and his therapists told Mom that Howie was getting worse, that he was a danger to us too and she should split. It was very tough but she got a divorce that crushed him, but she had to keep her boys safe. He left for good after that. I felt bad. He was a good guy but seeing so much shit in the war fucked with him. All the kids liked the guy even though he was socially awkward. He had a good heart. My mom took it hard because she just wanted us to have a normal family and this latest sitch was coming to an end.

Then one day, out of the blue, I got a bike in the mail. The tag said that it was from Sam Spade, my real dad. Shocking but I'll take it! Then, the next day, a couch showed up. Hmm. From Sam again! Double hmm. This guy hadn't given me anything more than a snow cone for ten years. WTF? Something was fishy. Then more shit appeared. It just kept coming. Soon enough, we got the news. Howard had used his hospital connections to make a fake ID to pose as my dad. He started sending us the shit Sam never provided for us when we were younger. Howard was so mad at Sam for ditching us, that this was his kooky way of helping us out while also getting back at him. Sam wound up getting thrown in jail until it was sorted out.

The police eventually figured out the fraud and caught up to Howard. They cornered him in a motel somewhere in the Midwest. He didn't give up; instead he quietly took the drugs he brought and killed himself. He had it all planned. It was pretty sad.

I found out later he had tried to take his own life once before with a shotgun, but my mom had knocked it away just in time.

That's when he blew the hole through the closet ceiling in our house.

A few years later my mom got so pissed at Sam that she finally talked a lawyer friend into helping her out to get some dough out of him. My dad hadn't paid a cent of child support or alimony in years. She could never do anything about it, because she was broke. So this lawyer friend got my mom her day in court. Sammy trotted in with his flip-flops, Lacoste shirt (collar flipped up), Bermuda shorts, and Carrera sunglasses. The judge said, "Are you Sam Spade?" "Live and in person!" he smarmily replied. "Is it true you never paid this woman a dime in all these years since leaving her?" the judge asked. "Well, it's tricky, Judge, you know how it is with the dune buggy payments and the brunches . . ." SLAM! (Gavel coming down, in case you were confused.) SIXTY DAYS IN JAIL! Sammy got dragged away. "Whhhaattt? What's happening?? I can't go to jail, I have a thing at noon. Come on, Judge, don't do this!! BE COOL! YOU'RE A GUY!!" Sam only did about two days (like Paris Hilton) but it was a good scare. Apparently all it did was scare him back into the bars looking for women to pick up, but at least Mom tried.

CHAPTER TWO

MAMA'S BOY

'm probably a total mess today because growing up, my mom was the only one around most of the time. And believe me, my mom did her best, I was really just a boy without a dad, drifting aimlessly through Arizona. Don't get me wrong, I had waves of seeming tough, but I didn't realize it. When I was ten and my brothers were twelve and fourteen my mom would sometimes drop us off at the end of the desert when she went to work and pick us up seven miles away at a Chevron station when she got done. This was only when she didn't have a babysitter and I'm sure done out of desperation. The funny part was she would also let us each bring a gun and ammo so we could shoot shit and have fun along the way. We had a rifle, a pistol, and a shotgun. But also a canteen, bag lunch, and Bactine (in case of emergency!). I never thought twice about this other than remembering it was really fun, and my brothers and

I had a blast. But, today some fuddy-duddies might consider this "dangerous." But down deep I was a mama's boy. As much as I wish it wasn't true it just happened. The things that dads teach sons, I never really learned. My mom loved to give us presents, but there wasn't a man around to tell my mom, "Hey hon, that's kind of a fruity gift for a kid, you know." Once HPH (Howard P. Hyde) was gone, the shotguns stopped appearing under the Christmas tree. And she's a mom and moms are chicks. And that's cool, but Mom didn't get the fact that for every female-slanted present you give a boy, you have to even it out with some solid manly gift. That's just the rule. Like for every set of socks or tighty whities, there needs to be a punching bag or a skateboard. One Christmas, she had a major brainstorm. "I'm going to take a school picture of each of the boys, and put it on something they can keep forever!!" (Zero logic, by the way. This reeks of something in SkyMall but there was no SkyMall back then. Somehow, in the seventies we managed to get by without a Bug Vacuum or Hot Diggity Dogger; go figure, so we didn't need SkyMall.) So, there's dear ol' mom, she went out and got us each a specific thing with our photo emblazoned upon it. Bryan got off easy. He got a coffee mug with his mug plastered on it. Not horrible, although he was fourteen and probably wasn't a major Sanka drinker to this point, but no biggie. Coffee mugs also hold Tang and Mr. Pibb, so he was fine. And, if necessary, he could bury it in the back of the cupboard and no one would be the wiser. Then came Andy's turn. He woke up Christmas morning and unwrapped a pillow with one whole side as his school head shot. Wow. None of us knew what to say. We all just stared at mom while she beamed. "Dontcha just love it?!" she said. Andy sort of shrugged thank you, knowing deep down this wasn't a great one for show-and-tell . . . because Andy and Bryan were tougher and more manly than me cause they had a little more of my dad.

Bryan is the dude who got in fights all the time, and he went to jail at fourteen, which I don't even think is possible anymore. He's also the dude who loves snakes and beer and tarantulas. Andy's not quite as Paul Bunyan as Bryan, but he's the dude who dressed cool, he had a cool bike, and he got girls two years older than him. So he knew right away that he had to bury that present in the closet, facedown so in the event anyone peeked in there they wouldn't see his smiling head shot.

Next was my turn. The mama's boy. The kid who slept in the same bed with her three years too long. The one who held her hand in public five years too long. This was me. Anyway, she was the most excited about this present. Her call for me was a white T-shirt with a huge picture of ME in the left corner. YES, FOLKS, ME. The picture was in a huge circle. Like monstrous. Underneath, it even said "Dave." Just so you wouldn't be confused that *this guy* was *this guy*. The room went silent. I held the shirt up. Even more silent than before. Finally my mom goes "It's a picture of you! On a T-shirt! That you can wear!" She squealed. In case it wasn't 100 percent obvious what this was, Mom had to make it extra clear. Surely she was concerned about our lack of reaction. Then she goes, "Wear it to school!" And I go, "I should! That might be fun!" because I was a little bit of a fruit, and I didn't know. I didn't want to hurt my mom's feelings, because I didn't have my dad around to say, "Fuck no, Judy, he's not wearing that!" (Another reason I'm pissed at my dad.) I just rode on Mom's wave of excitement. "Yeah, let's do it!" I literally did everything except make the snaps like the guys did on *In Living Color*. You know those 3 snaps, like a "Z".

So come Monday I'm about to go skipping off to school (not a total exaggeration, to be honest) and then somehow at the last millisecond my male chromosome somehow woke up and said to my brain, "Wait a second! Can we just throw a shirt on over this?

I mean, maybe just a little button-down? Just something in case, worst-case scenario, a selfie on your T-shirt isn't the coolest thing on the planet? Just . . . some sort of coverage. Just for me. The male part. I only pop up once a year. Throw me a crumb." I thought, Okay, fair enough. So I grabbed my button-down and headed out the door with my baton. No . . . seriously but, I almost had one, that's how unaware I was.

So I ride my bike to school. (Yes, helicopter parents, it's true and it worked just fine. Three miles! Oh yea. Never got kidnapped or raped. S'all good in the hood.) Now this being Arizona, and it was scorching during normal recess time, we played kickball for our first hour of the day. Arizona (Trivia!) folks. So I took a breather leaning against the backstop and I was like, "Wassup, gals, what's happening, ladies? How was your weekend?" Ya know, just kicking back with some small talk, the normal daily drill, little flirting, a little gossip. Catch up with everybody and in a flash, everyone was back to playing kickball. By the way, I'm actually pretty good at kickball. (I don't want to talk about that right this second but just FYI, I'm a little bit of an athlete . . . I mean you roll it down I'm going to kick it pretty hard, that is all I'm saying. Seriously, some guys bounce it, which is illegal, but either way I'm going to whack it. So if you're the pitcher, might as well roll it smoothly down to me so you can sleep at night because you won't be a cheater and either way you're going to get shelled. But that's neither here nor there.) So here I am, kicking back on the fence, taking five, and now it was time to make my move. I was ready to unveil the little Spade face on my shirt. This is such a true story it scares the shit out of me when I tell it because as I tell it, I feel the pain again. It feels like I'm having flashbacks to Operation Desert Storm. These were the last happy thirty seconds of my life. So I went to start to pop a few buttons, just open it a little bit, you know one button maybe two, just so there's a little tiny piece of my happening Farrah

Fawcett feathered bangs that were sticking out. I took a beat. No trouble yet, everyone's still playing the game, doing hopscotch, chillin' whatever. So I go, everything's cool. Pop one more button and started to take my shirt off. Was about halfway off my shoulder, and the entire school yelled, in unison, "QUEER!" I was like "woah." Oh my god I freaked out, having no confusion over who they were yelling at. I hauled ass back to homeroom. I buttoned my shirt on the way back so fucking fast my hands were a blur. I sprinted to my homeroom, dove under the desk, and had a full-blown panic attack. "OH MY GOD, OH MY GOD, ABORT MISSION!! THIS IS NOT A DRILL!!" My heart was racing in my tiny bird chest. My BP was like 10,000 over 50 million. Then, the entire school came pouring in, screaming "Holy shit! Spade's got a picture of himself on his shirt! This is unbelievable!!" "No I don't! No I don't!" I screamed. "I promise I don't!" And then I added this to make sure I was going to hell: "I SWEAR TO GOD I DON'T!"

I was totally up against a wall. "Yes, you do!" everyone screamed back, and then came my second horseshit defense. "They can't even do that! They can't even put a picture on a T-shirt. Did you hear what he said? That's crazy, he's saying crazy things!"

Meanwhile that's all they can do to T-shirts, is put pictures on them. I would have gotten killed in cross-examination.

I was out of my mind. So I sat there and they go, "We should put it in the time capsule . . . so in 2020 they can know what a fruitcake you were . . . for posterity."

Sad. But, I might dig that up. We should go dig that up.

CHAPTER THREE
LOSING MY VIRGINITY

t was my senior year of high school. Class of '82 ('82 drinks more brew!). (By the way, I wouldn't mention the exact ancient year that I graduated but with Google it's just a matter of time before chicks figure out my age. For a while I tried only to date girls who didn't have the Internet but that was too small of a pool.) I wish I had gotten laid sooner in high school, believe me. I had enough boners that went to waste to fill Cardinals Stadium. That's a huge stadium in Arizona. From roughly the sixth grade on I had a bone-anza of boners oh my god. (Side note to self: Copyright the word *bone-anza* for movies, books, T-shirts, and TV. [Side side note: not to be confused with TV show *Bonanza*.]) I had probably upwards of *hmmm*, ahh let me do the math (thinking out loud) 25 rods a day on school days, so times 5, and maybe 10 on weekends, bop bop bop . . . carry the 4 . . . equals 13.6 million pup tents. Of that number approximately 100 percent went to waste or were destroyed by any four pages of *Penthouse*. (Kaboom! Feel the rain on your skin . . . song from *The Hills*.) (Side note: Chicks in *Penthouse* were always somewhat sluttier/whorier than *Playboy*. Guys realize that at a young age. No one is marrying these gals, so they were smart to play that angle. They would also throw in a beaver-munching scene here and there to keep the customer happy. Oh it did. Very. With those scenes I only needed about three pages before shrapnel was flying.) With three boys, BTW, my house had dirty magazines stashed all over. Which made Easter mornings a bit awkward. But finally, at the not so tender age of seventeen, I got some real-deal sex.

Here's how the beautiful magic went down. Every year, this guys in this club I was in, or part of, called. The Gents (lame) . . . had a boxer party. We would each ask a girl to be our date and then we would go to the house of whoever's parents were away and party in our boxers. (Not overly clever but at least it seemed like a decent theme.) We'd get shitfaced and trash the place. This is also the basic premise for *Porky's 4* (I'm guessing; I've only seen the first three). For this year's boxer party, I asked a chick that I had a thing for. I had no idea if she dug me, though. She was actually pretty robotic, to be honest. Not tons of emotion or deep thoughts going on, but pretty and pleasant enough. That met all the criteria I needed. And she said yes. And she was a girl. Presumably with a pussy. So I was game. All the pertinent boxes were checked. Also, in full disclosure, this girl had been kind enough to cough up a hand job to me about six months earlier so we were already headed in the right direction. She had seen my dick and seemed to be okay with it, so we were in business. (By the way, my prong is nothing to write home about. It's sort of a shoulder shrugger.) We will get to that later.

I had pulled out my porksword for her. Nothing.

Crickets.

She just sort of shrugged her shoulders and started tugging, she was like starting a lawn mower you know. Not a ton of finesse happening, but I wasn't complaining. I could tell she got bored fast. Luckily we had no cell phones back then, or she would have been checking her Instagram feed the whole time. This amazing moment happened in the backseat of my buddy's car on the way to Flagstaff with my two buddies Joe and Steve in the front seat. When I finally "finished" (gross term) it looked like a paint can had exploded on my Lacoste dark blue shirt. I had not planned ahead. I just sat there. Didn't know what to do. There was no Shout-ing it out. I had to take a walk of shame into 7-Eleven and buy paper towels. (Ah, romance.) The 7-Eleven guy didn't flinch. I have a feeling this scenario had somehow played out before, and he had seen it.

So my robotic date and I walked to the boxer party from her house. At this point, I was still wearing pants. It was good that we walked, since I planned on getting hammered. Not that it would have mattered since there were no drunk-driving laws back then. (Can you imagine? A world where you don't get DUIs and you can drive shitfaced? Again back when America was great. Cops didn't give a fuck, they just told you to focus on the road before high-fiving you.) Anyway I hit the partay in my Brooks Brothers ironed all-cotton boxers a little crease in 'em. I was a preppy asshole at the time, by the way.

So, as all high school dates began, we immediately started playing quarters with shots of tequila. This is a dumb move because you get plowed so fast and you don't even get to build a good buzz, but what do I know at seventeen? My buddies and I just wanted to look badass in our boxers in front of these chicks. I was feeling especially awesome because I finally had a date. (My luck with the ladies was pretty limited at this tender age. I had yet to get on a TV show, which makes dates with me at least bearable.) Pretty soon I'd had about seven shots in me, and my date was going on her fifth. Things started getting flirty and touchy and in the background I hear that Journey song "Lovin', Touchin', Squeezin'." This is the Journey song I love. At the end of this song, Steve Perry goes "NA NA NA NA NANA, NANA NA NA NA, NA NA NA NA NA NA NA NA NA NA NA NAAAAA, NA NA NA," etc., ad nauseam (it actually never fucking ends) so I said, "Wanna get out of here?" or something equally cool and James Deany. And she is like, "Yea, yea okay." Or "Help," or whatever. I can't really recall.

So we head back to her place, which was a tough walk considering my rod, which is hard to hide in the boxers. Her parents were asleep so we go into her room. We kiss, major French action. (She wasn't a bad kisser but some high school chicks over-French when they kiss and it's gross. Not that I've kissed any high school chicks lately or anything.) Eventually, she fell back on the bed and I took this as a written invitation for some action Jackson. I start to pull on her boxers. (Oh yeah, chicks wore them, too. We were cool.) And she lifted up her hips! Now this is the best move in history. Every guy waits for this, because that means that she's helping, and she's into it, it's green-light city. Underneath the boxers of course she was wearing panties. Back in those days, this meant those serious mega-drawers. Like five inches of fabric on each side and about twenty in the dumper. And speaking of mega, her bush was sort of out of control, too. It puffed out so much that her panties looked like an airbag had gone off. None of this bothered me a bit, of course, because underneath that airbag was a vajayjay and my ween was hopefully headed for an air strike.

My boxers flew off in .04 seconds. I was so stoked, you cannot imagine. You probably can. We started kissing again and I slid my meat mallet in (I should write romance novels, next?) and she doesn't make a peep. No "Oh shit!" No "OMG, it hurts!" No "Just the first part!" No words at all, just a blank expression. She had the same glazed look as someone sliding their ATM card through the checkout thing at Kmart. Fine. I can't have everything. I block out her lack of super sexy turned on response and focus on the task at hand. And I'm in heaven. We start kissing, now she's getting into it, she's got her eyes closed, she loves it. I'm thinking, *This feels better than I thought! This is almost better than beating off! No wonder everyone's hooked!* But soon, the moaning stops I think she's zoned out. So I rode out the last eleven seconds in my own happy world and then blew fog all over her hips, hair, scrunchie, pillows, walls, carpet, beanbag chair, hallway, and part of the kitchen. Even her dog made that shake move so I think he caught some of that, too. Unfortch. Poor thing. But I'd been waiting for this day forever. My balls were like THIS IS NOT A DRILL!! And they came through. Big-time.

Once we were finished, my date looked at my ween and giggled. I think the sex came across as tickling to her which is not great. So we skipped the spooning, and now what do I do? I had no dad around so I knew nothing about sex or what to say after or before or at school or anything. My only thought was, How do I tell my friends? This is front-page news! Using her home phone might be tacky and plus there was splooge all over it. So I did what any gentleman would do. I put a blanket over her and tiptoed toward the door. Then I hear her say, "You'll get better at this" and she laughed. Ouch. Nothing stings like a bad Yelp review.

I drunkenly walked about two miles home. I was on cloud ten. I got in about 3 A.M. and crashed in the cruddy two-bedroom apartment that I shared with my mom and two brothers. I did kinda want to wake up Bryan and Andy and tell them, but I was worn out from all the sex, and I crashed. The next day I woke up and remembered what had happened. I was so happy. I sat over my Lucky Charms in total pre–high-five mode. Then, of course, I did the gentleman thing and started telling anyone who would listen about how I banged the hell out of this girl and how she loved every second of it. I couldn't wait for school Monday. Sunday night was like Christmas Eve. Couldn't wait for morning! I cruised around school like the town crier, all pointy boots and scrolls. "Here ye! Here ye! By proclamation of the king . . ." I never gave an ounce of thought as to whether or not the girl wanted to be on board with this publicity junket. Remember, I didn't have a dad around to explain to me that if I blabbed, other chicks wouldn't want to bone me. And Bryan and Andy didn't care if I got laid. So I started my junket, singing like a canary to anyone and everyone. That was a magical day, almost as good as the bone-down itself.

After she got word off this not only did she never do me again, but no other chick in high school wanted to be in my press release, either. Thank God there was no Twitter or Facebook then, or I would have been frozen out by chicks for the rest of my life. I didn't really understand why she got upset that I blabbed. I gave her great reviews! All the dudes now knew she was good in the sack! Four stars all around! But alas, no more action was coming my way for this little dirtball. What a bummer.

About ten years later I saw her again. I was back in AZ taking a victory lap cause I was on TV and wanted to bop around my old haunts and act like I hadn't changed. Even though I totally had. I was wearing this huge black leather Fonzie/Dice Clay horribly-fitting biker jacket that cost way too much. And weighed roughly fourteen pounds and actually hurt my neck. That already hurt. I looked like a fucking moron, but I wore it proud. The best part of this story was I kept walking around saying, "Everyone's changed, man." Even though I was the one who changed, and they hadn't at all. What an asshole. A few people I ran into mentioned at the club that I was a dick now and that I thought I was cool. I was like "Whatever, I've met stars." (Not exactly the best answer to erase those douchebag comments.) So I bounced from that club and headed to another. I kept repeating this new phrase to everyone: "This place is weak, *I'm gonna bounce.*" So I eventually bounced home. On the way home I stopped by Circle K. This is a convenience store chain, which is basically 7-Eleven. And when I say "basically" I mean it's exactly 7-Eleven. So I headed in to try to buy a six-pack before it's last call and lo and behold who is the pretty cashier but my very first bone-down! (No names here. I finally stopped ruining her rep.) So we chatted and flirted because apparently I was a bit more interesting now. She said I wasn't that bad in bed (a 6 out of 10!), so that made me feel good. She was very sweet. I guess fame makes you better-looking. But, as nice as it was to see her, that ship had sailed, and I wanted to maintain the memory of our one embarrassing moment together (mostly because I'm still no better at fucking and didn't want her to get that word out on the streets of Scottsdale), so we said our goodbyes. Her last visual of me is me walking out of Circle K with a six-pack of Heineken. Sort of hunched over, less from sadness and more from the enormous weight of my stupid fucking douchebag, new money, Hollywood jacket.

CHAPTER FOUR

MINI SPADE

When I was in high school I was mostly cursed with being the buddy of good-looking chicks. As previously mentioned, I got laid only once the entire four years of high school, despite the fact that my main mission from fourth grade on was to get laid every weekend. I gave myself freshman year to get my footing, and sophomore year was supposed to be for getting laid once a week. Then senior year every day. Well, it was all trickier than I thought.

Up until this moment, I had been the smart kid in school. Well, the desire to play chess, do my homework, and go to class was quickly replaced by the sudden thirsty need to be popular. *Popular* sounds like such an old-fashioned term now. In today's terminology, you could say that I wanted a lot of Facebook likes or Instagram followers. Of course, when you think about it, lots of followers on Instagram is even more of a bullshit illusion than friends in high school, because at least in school you physically see the people. Facebook is just fake connection, and if you ever delete your account and start over, half would never "like" you a second time. That's life on the mean streets of Facebook and everyone knows it. In high school you truly believe that all these people will be friends for life. And you're lucky if you keep in touch with two after graduation. But making those friends was super-important to me.

I figured high school would continue my long-standing trend toward nerd city, but a funny thing happened when I got there. My brother Andy was already there, he was a junior, and he was supercool. He had long brown hair that was blond on the ends from sun (yes, it's possible not to fake this) and he was tan, good-looking, and artsy. (The puss magnet trifecta!) So out of nowhere, just because I was related to him, word got around that I was cool, too! There's no definition for cool in high school, so it's hard to spot or argue against, and with such loose regulations I slipped through the cracks. I'll admit that I did have some of the components of a cool person. I had long white-blond hair, cool surfer shorts and shirts (even though I had never seen an actual wave at this point), and I could skateboard in pools. In fact, the week before freshman year started I broke both my wrists skating in a pool. I tried an aerial axle stall and fell backward into the deep end. So, on the first day of high school I waltzed in with a crispy white OP shirt from Miller's Outpost, turquoise cord shorts from Quiksilver, long feathered Farrah Fawcett hair, and two splints on my arms. From a distance, I seemed happening, but in person I had zero game. ZERO. I couldn't close any chicks. I talked too much, for one thing, and my subject matter was weak, mostly about coin collecting and how I fell easily off a skateboard, but still, the rumor of my coolness persisted. Meanwhile, all four grade schools had merged into this high school so everyone from my old school was saying, "Wait, you don't understand, he's a geek, he's a nerd, he hangs out with a Vietnamese kid!" But it was too late. All of Andy's hot cheerleader friends, juniors no less, took to calling me "Mini Spade" because they thought I was almost as cool as Andy. (Some of them were just nice to me to get in with Andy, which I spotted but was fine with.) Well, all the guys and girls from my freshman class picked up on this right away. They thought, Oh fuck, we had this kid pegged wrong! He *is* happening! The new coolness spread like wildfire. No one could stop it. Within a few days I was a 100 percent certified non-nerd, aka *the shit*. I adapted quite well to my new status. I'd even walk past the smart guys from my old grade school and rip on them: "Hey nerds, why don't you go do some flash cards? Hahahahahhhahahaa! Come on, new friends, let's hit the assembly." What an asshole.

But the problem was, I got a little too excited about this new-found social life. My grades started to slip because I spent less time doing algebra and more time at flower parties and football games or just bailing on class and getting stoned. We had two main factions at school: the freaks and the jocks. It was like a failed Apatow pilot. The freaks were the stoners. And jocks were jocks. Freaks basically got high out in the open, and most of the jocks got baked, too. But they hid it well and often wanted to beat up the stoners. I got along with both. I enjoyed toking away and tried out for sports, even though I wasn't exactly a star. I wasn't terrible, but I was never going to be a star. Or even pretty good. I went out for baseball and even football. I tried out for football my senior year, weighing in at a wispy 114 pounds; it was exactly like the movie *Lucas* . . . except not everyone liked me and clapped for me. I got pounded. I even had the balls to go out for basketball, just for something to do. The worst thing about that was when I got the ball in our practice games, the other team wouldn't even try to block my shots, and they would just sit back and yell, "Let him shoot!" This was even more humiliating because they knew that with absolutely no interference I would still miss. And I did. Every time. Obviously I got cut from all three teams, but at least I tried out. By the way, the freaks were restricted to only weed. It wasn't like today. We had no molly, no acid, no moon rocks, no crack, no coke, no special K, no codeine cough syrup, no Vicodin, no Xanax, no Adderall, no Klonopin. Nope, just booze and weed. Very basic. Like Kicking Wing in *Joe Dirt*. Snakes and sparklers. Not a big assortment.

I'm always asked if I was the class clown. I have to say no. I was sort of funny but I would whisper all my jokes to people in class. I wasn't the loud attention-getter. I think that's why the movies with Chris Farley seemed to work, because he was the typical loud class-clown type and I was quietly commenting on what was happening. That combo felt like it had a groove to it. It was a good pairing. I got that style by lack of confidence in my jokes. I felt if I said them quietly and with no spin on them, then it didn't count if I didn't get a laugh. I would just say that wasn't *a joke*, I wasn't trying, I was just stating something. Because if you really lean on a joke and it whiffs, you look like an asshole and it counts as a strike on your stats. I was more like the guy running for mayor. I was very social at this point, mixing it up with as many people as I could. Shaking hands, kissing babies. You know the drill. Hey, I'd been socially starved my whole life. Now I was experiencing a microlevel of fame. I'd been plucked from grade school obscurity to having folks know who I was. My mom was pissed about my report card shitting the bed, and Andy was annoyed that I was riding his coolcred coattails, but I didn't care. I always knew if things got bad I could easily turn into the skid and bust out a 4.0 overnight. Not a problem.

Turns out, it was a problem. My acceptance into Mensa got sidetracked by the idea of doing comedy. It was my sophomore year when I decided that I would try to be funny, not quietly at lunch but onstage.

In my Scottsdale, Arizona high school, one of the offered electives was a motivational speaking class. This was a pretty easy one for me, because it was a perfect way to show off. A lot of the class was learning how to give a speech in front of a group, which terrifies most people, but I seemed to like it (gross). THIRSTY! ATTENTION! A very sweet but stern older woman named Mrs. Nack taught the class. She was very good at getting the most out of you, and she didn't make things easy on us. I remember there was an "Ah" meter. Someone hit a bell every time you fuckin' said "Ah" or "Um" during a speech, which was great training because you would never guess how many times you say that in a conversation and how stupid it sounds. I wish there was a "Like" meter in every bar in Los Angeles or maybe even an "Amazing" meter for whenever a girl talks for more than five seconds.

This class was also my introduction to "the Light." The light is the famous red light on the back wall they flick on at the end of your stand-up routine. It means you have about two minutes to wrap it up. And I have learned through my stand-up career that a lot of places are not fucking around when they give you the light. I have gotten screamed at, and even fired on the road for not getting the fuck offstage when you get the light. Comics get a bad rap for going over on their time. Anyway back to speech class . . . If you had a five-minute speech, it was like a traffic light in the back: green went on when you hit three minutes, yellow for the fourth minute, then red for the last minute. We learned not to blather on, and try to keep it tight. If you've experienced my comedy stylings, you know I never blather on, well, rarely . . . well okay. Sorry, Mrs. Nack, I do it all the time.

The motivational part of this class involved a traveling team called Motivation in Motion, which consisted of a bunch of idiots going to grade schools and giving motivational speeches. Just picture Joel Osteen but younger, less religious, constantly stoned, and making absolutely no sense. That was us. It was almost comical how unqualified we were to be "motivating" but it was a fun way to get out of school for the afternoon.

Now, the main reason I took this class for three years was that Mrs. Nack had the keys to the kingdom. The Extravaganza. Extravaganza was a two-day, once-a-year talent/variety show. The whole school went, the whole school talked about it, and the only way you could get a slot on the program was if you were in the speech class. And I was so horny to get onstage at this point, ripping off old *Saturday Night Live* sketches, that I played all my cards with old Mrs. Nack. This was also the time that I first tried my hand at writing sketches. You will soon find out that I should have worked on that a little bit more, but in high school I was just getting started. I wrote a super-stupid sketch called "The Malachi Brothers," which was about two cocky guys hitting on women. It played pretty well, and with the positive feedback I got, I decided that comedy was maybe something for me. Sports and skateboarding weren't going to take me to the top, not even the middle. The sketches were super-stupid but they got me writing. And I couldn't rely on Andy forever. Comedy was the only place I could pretty much fit in and possibly stand out a bit. I still was into skateboarding with my brother, my friend Jody, and a handful of other burnouts, and no one cared about that. Performing was on campus, which made it more in the mix.

Unfortunately, writing practice and showing off wasn't the only thing I got at the Extravaganza. The first time I performed, it was sophomore year. It was a big deal I made the cut, because most of the slots were for juniors and seniors. This was my first vote of comedy confidence. (And I've been begging for pats on the back ever since.)

If you know me, you know I have a long history of neck pain and problems, and the Extravaganza is where they started. When I'm doing *Ellen* or *Fallon*, you'll see that I sit awkwardly on the couch, sort of cockeyed, or with my knees tucked under me. This is because I can't sit like a normal person for more than three minutes, because of what happened during my first Extravaganza. One of the sketches I was in was a dance number set to "Macho Man" (Remember that song? Very catchy.), and at the end of the dance number, I had planned to do a standing backflip . . . for no reason. Mostly just to show off, actually. As I tell this, I realize that there are a few red flags in this story but we're not going to focus on those. (Dancing, gymnastics, men everywhere, the term *macho man*. Ding ding ding.)

I was backstage before the show, going over my lines and dance steps. We were in the cafetorium, the combo cafeteria/auditorium where all the major shit went down. My buddy was there, decked out in his karate gi (he was also in "Macho Man"). I stupidly said, "Hey Williamson, can you spot me during my backflip, because I'm going to practice it?" And then, in a majorly regrettable move, I switched gears: "You know what? Don't spot me, I have to do it in an hour. I have to be ready." So his job was really to do nothing, just sit and watch the disaster unfold. I stood still and suddenly sprung straight up. After the flip I was supposed to land on my feet and stick the dismount like Mary Lou Retton. This did not happen. I came out of my tuck (lingo) a little early and I missed my feet, and landed on my FACE . . . yes, folks, all my weight, all on my face. There was a stunned pause; my friend stood there with his jaw dropped. Then I bounced up, holding on to my front four teeth, which were now bent straight back. Blood was squirting everywhere, and black paint from the stage was now tattooed on my teeth like a grill made out of Sharpie. "Are you okay?" my friend finally said. "Not at all," I reply, and as I walk away I hear music in my head. ("Hello darkness, my old friend"). I dropped to one knee, aaaaaaand . . . black out.

I eventually woke up, but for one solid hour I was laid out in the nurse's office at school, with no idea who I was. We're talking major concussion, people. By the way, when you get hurt in my family there's sort of an unwritten rule that you don't complain. You don't even say anything. When we were kids it was like we weren't allowed to get hurt, you know what I mean? I don't know if we even had insurance (we didn't) but around our house we had a "you're fine" policy. If anything at all went wrong, my mom just said, "You're fine." I'd go, "My stomach hurts . . ." "You're fine." "I fell off my bike . . . 'You're fine' . . . but the bone is sticking out . . ." "You're fine!" "Maybe I should see a doctor this time . . . ?" "YOU'RE FINE, DAVEY. A little Bactine will fix that right up!" Bactine is fake medicine, in my opinion. It just numbs things and bought my mom more time to think.

So, knowing I can't complain and may even actually get in trouble if I do, I was in a tough spot. I was in the school nurse's office and I didn't know what day it was, or who I was, for that matter. Then they brought my mom back, along with a doctor from the house. I didn't know my mom's name, but I sort of recognized her. Finally the old man doctor chimed in. "Well, he's a bit shook up." And I go, "Is that all you have? Are you from *Gunsmoke*? That doesn't mean anything! I have a category 200 concussion. I have amnesia! If I was in the NFL right now they would stop the game and chopper me out of the stadium. All the guys on my team would be down on one knee, freaking out. Even the other team would be on their knees like fake worried . . . Aw man, is he okay? Who cares, I'm going to rest a bit. (Pant, pant.)" (Even with a concussion I was doing bits.)

So the doctor looks at me again and this time said, "He's a bit rattled. Yeah, he got his bell rung." These are not medical terms, motherfucker! Finally, he said something that makes sense. "You better take him right to the emergency room." Well, Mom is a great actress. "Oh my God, of course!" Then the old doc scoots out and my mom leaned over and said, "Davey, do you want to go to the hospital or . . . PIZZA HUT?!!!" Oh my God, Pizza Hut?! They have Asteroids!!

So I never went to the hospital. I pushed all my teeth up in the right direction, so they felt even, and then put my retainer on (as painful as it sounds). Then months later the black paint fell off. So now if you ever see me on Kimmel and I'm wearing something that looks like a pukka shell necklace, now you know it's all Percocets. And I'm secretly chomping on them during commercials, "gnom gnom gnom, yummy fake puka . . ."

For the next year's Extravaganza I was even more ready to go. I had written more sketches this year. I had found that I was into this comedy thing, and I had spent the year since my unfortunate face-plant brainstorming ideas. This year things went better, save one tiny pratfall. The "Extrav," as we called it, was the Super Bowl for drama losers and wannabe comedians (and people who didn't roll their eyes when saying the word *Extrav*). The night of the show my friend and I had concocted a bit about two guys discussing fashion. One was dressed as a Lacoste alligator and the other as a polo player. They were onstage arguing over which brand was better, until the end, when I walked by in shorts and casually said, "Hey dudes, what's going on?" Then the other two guys yelled, "Oh no! It's the OP man!" and chased me off. (Hilarious? Maybe?) When we did it live, the polo guy swung his real wooden mallet at me and nailed me on top of the head as I ran offstage. By the time I got to the wings there was a dime-size dent in my noggin and blood was running down my face. I packed on the ice, but damn, it hurt. Didn't help the neck down the line, just so you know. But it got laughs so I wasn't mad about it. A lot of stuff we did in that show worked, which made me get even more into it the following year. At this point it never crossed my mind I'd be doing this shit forever. I never dreamed you could make money at these shenanigans. There was too big a gap between me and people on TV, so I wasn't even picturing that as an option.

The Extravaganza my senior year was a smooth ride. My friend Dan Minton and I wrote a ton of stuff, and a lot of it worked. Our friends called the show "Extrava-dave-and-danza" that year, which was a burn but that was fine because I didn't get hurt and I was on to something with this comedy biz. I had the bug. (Turned out to be Ebola.)

But then the year was over, and everyone was leaving for college. Shit. What do I do now?

Mini Spade needed a plan.

CHAPTER FIVE

JOINING A FRATERNITY

The time had come to think about college. I'd been putting this off forever. All my friends had a plan. I was literally the only one who didn't have some idea what to do after graduation. It wasn't like my mom had the time or the energy to sit me down and say, "Now Davey, you need to study for those SATs so you can get into the Ivy Leagues." She was too busy working to pay the light bill. My brothers and I had to take matters into our own hands. So, at the end of my senior year, I waltzed into the office of my guidance counselor (whom I hadn't talked to in years) and said cockily, "I'm torn between going to Princeton or UC Santa Barbara. Help me pick." These were the two schools I had been thinking about back in seventh and eighth grade, back when I was killing it in every class and was king of the nerdlies. At this point, I haven't even thought about college since I saw *Animal House* freshman year. But I'm still fully confident that Princeton and Santa Barbara are on the table and waiting for my nod. The guidance counselor looks at me and says, "If I pull some strings I might be able to get you in the community college across the street."

Ummm, not the answer I was expecting . . .

In my head I was thinking, *WTF, lady, I'm a genius. I'm not going to some dogshit community college. It'll kill my game!* Not to mention my mom would quietly cry because I had the one chance in the family to break out of the hood with a real school. (Hood being the section of Scottsdale for folks who made less than $150,000 a year.)

So I got into Scottsdale Community College. You knew it wasn't Princeton because our mascot was named the Artichokes. It would be funnier if I hadn't gone there. Everyone else had scrammed across the country and I was stuck driving three miles away to a college on an Indian reservation. It was a little bleak for the kid who read forty-seven books in sixth grade. The first thing I did as a college student was to sign myself up for early classes to make sure I didn't party too hard: 7:30 A.M. classes on Monday, Wednesday, and Friday. If I was going to go to community college, I was going to be the top community college student ever. It was time to get serious again. Time to start a self-discipline plan. What a fucking mistake that was. Way too aggressive. I dropped that 7:30 class within three weeks. I was already worried less than a month in that my GPA wouldn't be as robust as I wanted it to be. I was smart enough to take tennis at night, and I did pretty well in that, except I couldn't picture any future employers getting excited over that class. "I read here on your résumé that you get your first serves in a lot . . . you're hired!" None of my high school friends were around anymore, and this was a real wake-up call for me. You get spoiled in high school because there are always ten people around to meet up with or have lunch with or hang out with. Suddenly it's just crickets, because everyone I knew who was with me at this crappy community college was not someone I wanted to hang out with, and I'm sure they were thinking the same thing about me. (It was like the old Woody Allen joke, "I'd never want to belong to a club that would have me as a member.")

Early in my first semester, I made a small blunder. (Not to be confused with the old robot show *Small Wonder*.) I'd head back over to high school and sit on the wall by the cafeteria after my classes ended for the day. It didn't occur to me how desperate that was, until one day a few of the seniors came over and started chatting me up. "Hey, dude, what's going on? Don't you have class to go to? In college?" I'm like, "Dude!" "I picked my own skedj, and I made sure I was tapped out by eleven thirty in the A.M. It's perfect because I can come over here and have lunch." The guy was like, "Remember how Perkins and Stiller used to come back and sit on the wall after they graduated and we thought it was kind of a loser move?" I would chuckle, "Yeah what a bunch of those losers can't believe they did that. Get a grip, guys, like move on, high school's over." And then I just stared at the parking lot oblivious to the fact that they were trying to tell me something.

One night I was randomly looking through the local newspaper, the *New Times*, and I saw an ad for a comedy night. I thought it might be cool to go watch. Then I noticed that they also hosted an amateur night. I sort of missed the old Extravaganza days, so I thought maybe I could write down a little comedy act and give it a whirl. I went down to watch. First, I checked out the amateurs a few days later, and they were horrible. I had the confidence that I could be just as horrible. So the next week, I got some balls and went down and tried five minutes of material. I was eighteen and terrified. I had only seen comedians perform on Johnny Carson's show or cable specials, never in person. I didn't really know what a "club" comic actually did. First I figured I could just go onstage and repeat jokes I had seen Eddie Murphy or Billy Crystal do, because I memorized their HBO specials. It never crossed my mind that that would be considered stealing. To me it was just like being in a cover band singing the hits of Journey or the Rolling Stones. I was simply paying homage. But I decided against this approach. I went down to that club with my crummy scribblings.

I was the youngest guy who hit the stage that night. I looked about eleven. Some of my killer jokes included, "You know when you walk barefoot over someone's yard and it is made up of gravel and rocks?" (Believe me, in Arizona this is a real thing. There is very little grass around. It is all just cactus and small rocks.) "Well, here's my impression of someone walking across that yard." And then I'd walk daintily, lifting my hands in pain and say, "Ow! Fuck! Shit!" (Cue silence.) Later I changed the joke to, "You know when you get a small rock in your shoe and every time you take a step, it moves to a different part of your foot so that the people see you walking going . . . 'Ow! Fuck! Shit!'" (Sort of the same joke, but better premise.) "You know when you squirt mustard in your liverwurst sandwich and the first four gallons are yellow water? I'm like gross! Where's the mustard? Good night, folks!"

It's a shame I wasn't discovered that night, with such solid material. The club manager came up to me at the end of the night and said, "Your material was shitty, but what you said in between jokes was funny. Do more of that. You can come back." This guy didn't realize it but with one passing comment, he sort of summed it all up and really nailed it. The rest of my life, the best stuff for me would be those throwaway jokes. That's what would keep me alive in comedy. But it took me a while to figure it out. This dope nailed it in four minutes.

I started hitting all the amateur nights around Scottsdale. Some would even slide you twenty dollars' gas money at the end of the night. I quickly did the math and thought, if I could get four paying gigs a week, I'd have eighty dollars a week. Then I could quit my job, quit school, and become a pro comic. Full-time!

In between amateur nights, I went to a club called Chuckles and saw my first actual, professional headliner, a guy named Barry Sobel. I couldn't believe how fucking funny he was. He was so fast and had such tight material. I knew that if I could ever pull together an hour of material that good, I'd be on my way. Right now, that was sort of beyond my comprehension, an hour of good shit. So maybe quitting school wasn't the best course of action after all.

The following year I got into Arizona State University. See you later, Shitty Community College; let's stay friends! I had no money, a crappy car, and a room in a bleak little apartment. I had a job at a clothing store where my brother Andy and his girlfriend Katy worked. Andy ran the men's side. Katy ran the women's. Later they would start dating and create KATE SPADE handbags and get rich and famous. (That's another book . . . a better one.) But for the time being, we all had these normal jobs and lives in Arizona.

Getting into ASU was a huge upswing in my social life. Andy, my cool brother, was in a fraternity called SAE. Sigma Alpha Epsilon. This was the preppy, douche frat on most campuses but at ASU this was the coolest one. They glommed on to me right way, because I was Andy's little brother, and asked me to join. I was so flattered. I went through rush week getting my ass kissed. I had a hunch this was too good to be true and yet, I still fell for this act. All week they were telling me that I was special, that they'd be honored to have me as a brother. Like a moron, I believed it! So, I signed on to be a pledge. This was a mistake. The second rush week was over, all of the pledges were gathered into a room where the brothers began screaming at us, telling us what losers we were and that we were to address them saying, "Yes, sir, sir, active sir" at all times because we were pledges or "plebes" and they were the almighty "actives." I did this bullshit for six months. It was shocking at first, even though I sort of should have known it was coming. I'd seen every fraternity movie and they always treat the pledges like shit. I had been thinking that these were the greatest guys I'd ever met. I got so bamboozled. Where were the cool guys who were kissing my ass? I sort of wanted to pull them aside and say, "I get the Dr. Jekyll and Mr. Hyde routine but it's a little tired and frankly a bit corny so maybe let's get back to that rush week attitude and why don't you fetch me a beer?" These are the kind of comments I was too scared to say to the actives but would whisper to the pledges.

Eventually, the whole fraternity found out I was sneaking off and doing comedy nights around town. This gave me a tiny bit of coolness factor, especially when we had mixers with the sororities. My favorites were the DGs (the dick grabbers), Gamma Phi Betas (the Goo-Foo-Boos), the Gamma Phi's (the grab-a-thighs), and the Alpha Phi's (the all-for-frees). They were all hot in my mind, and during rush week I had been told I could fuck any one of them if I just pointed at the one I wanted. An active would simply bring her to me. Of course, the story now was that none of the sisters would ever sleep with me because I was a loser pledge and besides, I wasn't allowed to talk to them, and P.S., go scrub the toilets you plebe fuck.

So now my life consisted of four things—working at the clothing company with Andy and Kate, doing shitty stand-up gigs at night whenever I could, being an SAE pledge and eating shit at every turn, and last and what turned into least . . . going to school. The pledging, or as they called us, "being a funk," took up 90 percent of my time. I had to report in and do chores around the frat house. (CHORES, FOLKS! LIKE I'M SEVEN!) By the way, you were not supposed to call it a frat house; you were not even supposed to call it a frat . . . the actives got very angry. They would always yell, "It's a fraternity! You wouldn't call your country a 'cunt,' would you?" That was their big line. It was sort of funny and logical actually, but I still called it a frat all the time. Don't get me wrong, there were some pluses to being in a fraternity; it definitely forced you to make friends fast. And we were drunk most of the time. Plus, we went through so much shit that it was like we were bonded for life. We were brothers, like vets from Nam. (I wonder if people who were actually in the Vietnam War get sick of this analogy. I use it all the time. I go to a bathroom in a gas station and come out saying, "It's like Vietnam in there." I don't think a bunch of spoiled Scottsdale boys running around with their shirts off, drunk, trying to fuck DGs, is an exact mirror image of seeing your three friends killed next to you in the real Vietnam War . . . but I'm going to keep using the analogy.)

The downside of being a pledge was that it sucked a lot of the time. My schoolwork was fading fast, my job was getting pissed at me for coming in drunk and/or super-tired, and the comedy nights were tough because I had classes at night, too, so I had to squeeze gigs in between. I pretty much felt like shit for five months straight. I didn't live in the frat house, so it was even worse for me because the older brothers would get drunk and call us in the middle of the night to come down for what was known as a "lineup" or "work party." I don't like *party* being after the word *work,* ever. In this context, you'd get a call at 4 A.M. and be told to go fetch river rocks from the dried-up salt riverbed and bring them to the house, or to come and do push-ups until they arrived. It was all such a mind fuck . . . but the biggest mind fuck of all was Oscar. We learned about Oscar our first day as a pledge. Oscar was a pig, and he was the SAE mascot. We were informed that the worst pledge of the semester would be fucking Oscar the night we became active. Yes. You read that right, folks! Fucking a pig! This was something I was *positive* had not come up during rush week.

To get assigned the Oscar fucking duty, which felt like a fate that could befall any of us, at any time, you had to be the worst pledge. That felt like a pretty easy task, based on the feedback we had received so far. At two in the morning, with beer being poured on my head, I'd be screamed at for what felt like hours. "FUNK #1, you worthless piece of shit! You know you're going to get Oscar! You homo! You want to bone a guy, pig! You want Oscar! You fag, you dream about Oscar!"

And I would sputter out a mouthful of Coors Light, "Yes, sir, sir active, sir."

"What? So you want to fuck Oscar?"

"No, I didn't understand . . . the question."

"Funk #1 wants to fuck Oscar!!!"

Then all the actives would make pig noises. "Oink, oink, oink." On and on it went. It's comical now, twenty years later. But when you're in the front lines of Nam and you're really in the (pig) shit, and you've got paprika on your head and baby oil all over your body and spray-painted button on your chest that requires you to quote a certain line every time an active pushes it, all of this seems normal. BTW my particular quote was "Lordy, I'm so tired, how long can this go on?" To answer my own question, it went on for the full semester.

Sometimes we served them dinner at night (WE SERVED THEM DINNER, FOLKS!), the drunkest one would decide to get little Spade on the little two-foot-high fireplace and say, "Do your fucking jokes, comedian. Dance for us, you clown." And I would get up and do some sort of shitty act and they would bitch that I did the same lame shit the last time they asked me. And I would fire back, well "I'm not exactly on a yacht in the south of France writing new material. I'm usually in the shower trying to get paprika out of my pubes." But, of course, I didn't say that.

You might be asking yourself where is my lovely, loving brother

Andy was during all this hellish process. Well, he wasn't exactly telling his brothers to go easy on me, his actual brother. In fact, he turned on me a few times when I was a plebe. One time I was in a lineup and all the pledges were drunk and beat-up from doing push-ups and getting screamed at as the actives walked around casually sipping drinks and barking out orders. Andy, who was an active, walked by me and whispered, "How you holding up, bro?" And I go, "Not great." And he goes, "You want some ice cubes?" "Yeah," I mumbled. He casually turned and screamed to the entire room, "THIS PUSSY WANTS ICE CUBES. FUNK #1 THINKS HE'S SPECIAL. EVERYONE DOWN AND DO PUSHUPS, HE THINKS HE'S BETTER THAN YOU." So everyone did push-ups while I sat there and ate ice cubes and felt their hatred, and I was like these icecubes are fucking awesome.

The other time he burned me was the one-in-a-million time in the mix when I got to leave with the prettiest girl there . . . a five-foot-ten DG who was featured on the ASU calendar. They called her "Wheels." For some reason Wheels was flirting with me this particular evening, and I was freaking out about it. I thought this might be my one chance to get laid that semester, as we headed back to her dorm. Her dorm was literally about a hundred yards away, but being a gentleman I am, I piped in with "I'll drive us." So, we got in my '72 Volvo and pulled out of the SAE parking lot shitfaced . . . I got pulled over within five seconds. I gave the copper my ID, but he didn't even bother, once he saw it he just yanked me and cuffed me. I started begging. "This is my one chance with Wheels. I don't know why I'm going to jail . . . please just let me slide this one time . . . please, let me catch a break." Wheels waved to me and started walking home. I was like wait for me. The cop told me I had a warrant for my arrest, which was news to me and I went in and spent the night in jail and a comic came and bailed me out. Turns out Andy had a pile of speeding tickets, which he had signed my name whenever he got pulled over. Because *he* didn't want to go to jail. When I called him on it, he didn't even really care. Thanks, bro. I slowly started to realize that my only true chance of getting laid my first semester at ASU was with Oscar.

There was something great that came out of my SAE adventures. Every year there was a big show called "Greek Sing." It was similar to Extravaganza, but bigger and better, and you had to be in a fraternity or sorority to participate. It basically involved big song-and-dance numbers, but in between the acts there were ten-minute breaks when a solo act would come out and sing, play the piano, or do something else. I decided that I needed to be one of those acts. So I gathered up the kit I had put together for my comedy gigs, which consisted of a Tom Petty hat, a little blue suitcase, a toy xylophone (for my *Jeopardy!* theme bit, aka hilarious!), my Casey Kasem impression, and the rest of my shenanigans, and auditioned for it. Yes, I was sort of a prop act at the beginning. I can't keep hiding this fact. Anyway, when I found out I made it in, I was ecstatic . . . until the nerves kicked in. As the night got closer, I kept thinking, *What the fuck am I doing?* I was backstage, listening to the cheers for all the songs from the three thousand people in the audience, and I almost couldn't take it. I felt super-sick. Every pretty girl in the Greek system was in the room watching. Every guy who hazed me, every person that I would see at any party for the next three years was out there, and in the next ten minutes they were going to decide whether I was cool or not. When I found out no one had ever done a stand-up act at Greek Sing before, I nearly left the auditorium. I went in the bathroom to wipe the sweat off before I went onstage, and I made a deal with myself. I decided that if I went out there and bombed, I'd quit comedy. My life was too hard at college as it was, and I couldn't take the physical toll of worrying about this shit anymore. *If I bomb, I will stop.* That was my thought, and it made me feel better because in ten minutes I would be able to quit, because I knew I was going to bomb. And then . . . they introduced me.

"From Sigma Alpha Epsilon, David Spade."

I got a polite smattering. The applause stopped before I got to the microphone. Bad sign. I think I used the old "How's everybody doing?" to get things rolling. I heard one guy say, "Bad." *Strike one.* Then I took the mic off the stand and said, "Can you hear me?" I hadn't done a sound check and I didn't realize that the crowd was absorbing most of the sound. I heard "No." Shit. Already off to a rocky start.

I mentioned something about going to the DMV, how much I hate it, and some people laughed so I relaxed a little bit. I did my second joke and more people laughed and realized I was doing stand-up and the crowd decided to give me a chance. People stopped talking. The third joke killed and I was off and running. I probably did eight minutes that day, and they were the most memorable eight minutes of my life, because that was when I decided that I would do comedy forever. I got offstage and I was on cloud ten. I couldn't believe how excited I was. I felt exactly 180 degrees opposite of before I went on. It was fucking great. I did something right.

From then on, everyone around town knew I was a comedian. People on campus started coming to shows to see me. Guys walking by me at school would give me a nod. That night was the single best thing that I got out of the Greek system. I see people now on the street who have read that I was in SAE, and it's always funny because they like to stick their hand in from a crowd of people and slip me the secret handshake and give me the wink as if I'm going to let them and their ten friends backstage. They think it is the handshake that separates them from the rest of the crowd, and it usually does because I do give those guys a little extra time out of nostalgia; some guys are really, really into being an SAE brother. And some are actually very cool. Everyone gets something different out of the Greek system but it just didn't resonate that much with me because once I went active they said, "You've made it through the hardest part; now you get to do it to the next guys." And I thought, I don't want to do it to the next guys, it's too fucking mean. That was tough mentally and physically to get through—a job and school and pledging (I didn't have money like the rest of them) so it wasn't just a party. I had to get something out of school. I had nothing to fall back on and I didn't have a dad and the family biz to fall into once I graduated. I wouldn't do it to the next guys. I actually wound up dropping out of all of it right after that, and doing stand-up full-time. I have some fun memories of my time with that crew, but ultimately Greek Sing was the thing that meant the most and changed the direction of my life more than college itself.

So now I was a "comedian."

CHAPTER SIX
GETTING SOME HEAT

I had been doing stand-up, kicking around the clubs for about seven years, when I got my first and only appearance on *The Tonight Show*. With Johnny Carson. I somehow snaked on two months before he retired. In my business you hear a lot of stories about the lucky or big break that launches someone's career. And those do happen. But for me, the whole thing was a lot more gradual, and this helped keep me sane. I hated the pace of my career at the time, because I'm super fucking impatient, but fast fame would be hard to handle. My slow, incremental rise to medium fame was easier to deal with mentally. I feel like people who get famous very quickly can't deal with the plethora (is that a word?) of shit that comes their way. Money, how everyone treats you differently in public, how your friends and family act toward you, etc. etc. I'm not sure people like the Kardashians would be more normal if they hadn't been on TV at a young age but they couldn't be any more nuts so I'm guessing fame did affect them. Also, if you are using a talent you have focused on your whole life at least feel like it paid off and you deserve the success in a tiny way or at least some attention for your work. But when you're on a show where the talent is arguing in the kitchen with your family, I'm guessing you feel like, Why the fuck am I a big deal? Cause you have nothing to point to (except selfies). Now back to my story. I can't pinpoint the one break that made the most change for me. I'm sure most people would point to *Saturday Night Live*. That's obvious. But I wouldn't have gotten to *SNL* without a lot of smaller things going right for me along the way. So, each of those mini breaks was very important at the time. And at the time of each one of those things was the greatest thing that ever happened in my life. So they all seemed huge.

The first break I got was when I tried to get in to the Los Angeles comedy club scene. This was after doing stand-up for about two years in Arizona. In Arizona, my big break had come when I got a slot in a bar called Anderson's Fifth Estate when I was only nineteen. They had a comedy night every Tuesday, and I eventually became a regular. My friends would often come out and see me. I also won third place in a comedy contest at ASU one year. (I know. Third place. Why am I bragging about it. I got a little whiff of micro-fame after my bronze finish. When I was packing up my Tom Petty hat and xylophone, a smoking ASU babe who was clearly out of my league was digging the fact that I placed in this half-assed contest. She came home with me and boned me for no apparent reason. I don't know if it was my UPS joke or my DMV bit that got her soaked but I do know that the downside was this was also the first time I smelled a rank beaver. Don't crash your car. It was brutal. I won't elaborate cause I'm a gentleman but it was like a bug bomb went off in my room. It was super-uncool. Naturally, I never mentioned it to her, because I'm immature, and besides there's really no way to break that news without devastating a woman. Hallmark hasn't really cracked the code on this subject. Believe me, I scoured the aisles at CVS for the perfect card to deliver that news.

When school wrapped up that year I decided to head to L.A. for the summer, because I thought I might be ready for the comedy scene out there. My mom had gone to California to work for some multilevel marketing scam company. She was a writer for their magazine and got me a job there. The whole thing felt like a big scam to me, but I needed the dough. And plus, what do I care? So from eight to five I spent my time filing stupid shit and plotting my comedy career. The only drug I could afford to numb my boredom with was Dexatrim. (For those of you under forty, Dexatrim was an over-the-counter medication marketed for weight loss. It was more like speed. Think of it as the Adderall for the Eighties.) Just so I could stay awake during boring filing. I know filing sounds glamorous but it's actually shitty. Showbiz had to wait . . . at least from 8 to 5 P.M.

I was aware of a few comedy clubs in town. The Improv and the Comedy Store were the most famous. There were some other places, but these were the biggest, the seven-nights-a-week places that I wanted desperately to crack in to. They each had an amateur night, too, and I decided the Improv was my best shot. I drove down to the club one night with my crummy little shoe box of props. I had decided that if I passed the audition, I could try to get maybe two or three spots a week and then I could afford to move out to Los Angeles permanently. I put my stupid name in a stupid hat, and waited. I sat in the back of the club, in my dumb outfit. (I had an old Batman sweatshirt, tight jeans, and Reebok high-tops. The same thing a girl would wear. Batman signals comedy, I guess?

I dunno.) The booker would pull seven names at a time, and each time a name was called my stomach would tighten up and I would sweat a little more, in panic that I would get chosen next. And I'd have to go right on stage. I sat there like a dope, waiting from eight to midnight, watching the crowd dissipate, I never got called, and then I had to leave because of the dogshit 8 A.M. filing job. My first trip to the Improv was a total bust. I realized pro showbiz would have to wait a little bit longer.

I went back home to Arizona with my tail neatly placed between my legs and I did stand-up in Arizona again, then I hit the road for another few years to get better. That Improv disaster scared me off of L.A. for a bit. Then a comedian I had met named Fred Wolf got me a show at the San Diego Improv, opening for a comedy team called the Funny Boys with Jonathan Schmock and Jim Vallely. They were hilarious. Fred was a comedian who was cool to me when he saw me go on in Arizona. So he helped me. He was a traveling road comic and threw me a bone because he liked my act. (On a side note we stayed friends. Later he worked on *SNL* and we wrote *Dickie Roberts* and *Joe Dirt* together.) The Funny Boys were great. Super-cool, super-hilar. They told me I needed to come back to L-A-A-S-A-P. They were talking to me in letters, I didn't quite understand. I listened to them because they were a great comedy team they had been on TV shows and even worked as writers on some (also; trivia alert: Jonathan famously played the maître d' in *Ferris Bueller*). Jim even said I could crash on his couch for a while. My response? "Fuck yes."

I drove out west in my crummy red '72 Volvo a week later. I somehow ran into Louie Anderson soon after I arrived, and he told me he could get me an audition at the Comedy Store. Louie was an even bigger deal. He was a regular at the Comedy Store and had been on Carson as well as many other shows. So I was sitting pretty this go-round in the big city. I had three legit comedians vouching for me and all I needed was one of these places to say yes. Either one would have been a major step for me in terms of becoming a pro comedian. Since there was such a rivalry between these clubs, you didn't get to play both unless you were a major pro. I wasn't gunning for anything like that. One would have been just great, thanks.

So, this time I headed to the Comedy Store, a hallowed place famous for launching the career of Richard Pryor and so many others before me. The woman in charge there is named Mitzi Shore, and she is notoriously tough. Plus she's Pauly Shore's mom, but that's beside the point. I thought I had a tight six minutes to showcase for Mitzi. I wasn't as crazy nervous as I had been that time at the Improv a few years back. I had finally ditched the props (thank God). I was ready. Louie came up and told me that I was on in twenty, so I hit the bar to have a drink and get my set together in my head. Only now, the stress was starting to get to me and my head started pounding. I threw back two Anacin tablets (or something equally dated, maybe Bufferin). Now here's where it gets interesting.

This situation was so stupid, yet I remember every detail. I had only about an inch left in my Greyhound (vodka and grapefruit juice) when I tried to chase down my dry old-school aspirins. Well, they didn't go down. And I choked. Then I ran to get water. Then I tried to hawk it up because one was now stuck in my throat. That didn't work, either. Then, somehow, the aspirin moved up into my sinuses and was burning. I sniffed and hawked and after a few minutes it came flying loose in a massive loogie. So disgusting, and such a project. Now I was exhausted and my heart was beating from fear of dying and my headache was twenty times worse. All of a sudden . . . I got called to the stage. For the first five minutes of my adult life I hadn't been thinking about comedy. I was just trying not to die. Now I realize I lived through this fucked-up sitch, but at the time I had to change gears really fast and do the most important audition of my life.

You can probably guess how this story ends.

I did my dopey little act for Mitzi Shore before a modest crowd of forty or so and then scampered out front on Sunset to wait. Louie came out a few minutes later.

"She's passing. Sorry."

"Holy shit." What a horrible feeling in my gut. Could I be way off? Do I suck? "I thought I did pretty good. No major fuckups."

"She liked your stage presence, but she doesn't think you're ready. Sorry."

Silence. I just stared. Then I said, "Cool. Cool. Okay . . . um . . . ya, well, thanks for setting it up, sorry it didn't work." (Trying to sound undevastated.)

I drove home in a daze. Holy fuck, one of the key puppeteers of my career just said no. What the hell was I going to do?

Turns out I didn't have too long to figure it out. I had to go to the Improv. This was my second and last hope.

The Funny Boys had set up an audition so this time around I didn't have to wait in line on amateur night with my props in a shoe box and my name in a hat. That meant I had to be ready to perform, because if they passed I couldn't audition again for another six months. And when I did, I would already have a stink on me from getting passed over. I was staying on Jim Vallely's couch, and every night I was quietly freaking out as my audition crept closer. I am overthinking my act completely. I couldn't really practice because no one will put me on. So I said it out loud in the bathroom, in the mirror, and I can safely say, it wasn't killing.

The night of my audition, we all headed down to the club. I was twenty years old, not quite twenty-one. I looked fifteen. The chalkboard outside the club included the name of the evening's performers, and for the first time, my name was up there. I had gone there so many times to hang out, to have a drink and try to catch a glimpse of the great comedians I had seen on television so many times—people like Jay Leno, Paul Reiser, Jerry Seinfeld, Kevin

Nealon, and Dennis Miller. All on the lineup. They all seemed to be about thirty-five, which to me was the oldest age I could think of at that time. I thought my only chance was that I was twenty with long white-blond hair and a lot of my jokes were about looking young. That would set me apart because Reiser, Seinfeld, and Leno all had a sort of similar "comedian" look, in my eyes. So I tried to use my different "Arizona" look to help me stand out.

I think that night I opened up with "Hi, I'm David Spade and I'm ten." That would usually get a laugh. Then I held up ten fingers and said, "That's this many. My mom just dropped me off. She's at Safeway. She'll be back to pick me up at nine." The set went well, and I went back into the bar super-adrenalized because I thought I had a chance of getting a weekly spot there. We sat at a big table and then one of the Funny Boys got word I passed, so we ordered a round of shots. Bruce Willis happened to be there that night and knew the guys so they invited him to join us. I was shitting my pants then because I was sitting with Bruce Willis. I almost forgot about making the Improv, until the waiter came back with the booze.

After he handed us the shots he said, "Wait, I need to see this guy's ID." This was the biggest needle scratch moment. Obviously I didn't have it with me. I mean I did, but it said I was twenty. So in a major buzz kill move, he took the shot back. All the fun was sucked right out of the moment, and a heap of embarrassment packed on top. But on the bright side, I was going to be getting regular spots at the Improv now. Then it hit me . . . I was going to have to move to Los Angeles.

Shit was about to get real.

I flew home and told my mom. She had moved back to Scottsdale after the L.A. job wrapped up. She was happy for me, but scared about things like where I was going to live, how I was going to eat, you know, important issues that didn't cross my mind. But the window was open for me and I had to go for it. And in a stupid move, I sold my car for the money that I would need to get started in L.A. and in a *stupider* move, I sold it to my brother Bryan, who said he would send me the cash but never did. And in the *stupidest* move, I am now in L.A. without money or a car. All I have is two twenty-minute spots at the Improv for thirty-five bucks a pop. Jim Vallely told me I could stay on his couch again, and thank God he did. He also had an old girlfriend who rented me a car for eighty dollars a week. (I was already ten dollars over budget.) The car was an old light blue Dodge Dart with three on the tree, which means it was a stick shift but the stick shift was on the steering column, so it was hard to drive. I knew how to do it from my old valet days. It had a crack in the windshield, the works. But I loved it. I ran out of money pretty much in a week. Jim told me I could have the change he kept in a jar so I took it down to Ralph's for a rotisserie chicken. I went home and doused it in my favorite A-1 steak sauce. Yummy. The Improv would let you eat there on nights when you had gigs, but you had to sign for your meals, which meant that when check day came around I'd be looking at a grand total of five dollars. It was lean stuff, very survival mode, very Bear Grylls. But I was getting spots onstage, and that's all that really mattered.

After I spent another weekend on his couch, Jim had had enough of me, and he told me that he had a friend going to England who would sublet me a studio down on Stanley and Santa Monica Boulevard. This, I found out later—and I was literally the official last one to find out—was a very gay neighborhood. Being from Arizona, I would parade down to 7-Eleven and back with no shirt and Quiksilver shorts. Every day, all day . . . like a little Joe Dirt in training. There were a lot of wolf whistles that I certainly never picked up on. But my most memorable night in that studio was spent lying on the futon on the floor (it was sort of no frills at this place) and listening to a woman scream bloody murder next door. I didn't know if they were having sex or he was killing her.

(I've never heard girls get loud during sex; whenever I look down at them they just say "Continue.") I lay down there missing Arizona, and all my friends hanging at my mom's house. All I could think was, What if something happens to me? I don't even know where a hospital is! I don't know anyone. I don't have health insurance. (Such a pussy.) Then the screaming escalated and I was terrified. I picked up the phone to call 911 . . . but I couldn't do it because I thought they would know it was me and would come kill me. So I got a huge knife from the kitchen and I sat on the bed, facing the door and holding the knife. I was ready to kill whoever came in. I was also scared shitless. The sun came up around 7:30 the next day and I woke up. I had fallen asleep on my side with my face on the knife. All that drama and I could have died by stabbing myself in the fucking face while I was sleeping. Who knows if she lived or died, that girl, it actually never crossed my mind again.

One day, after a few sets at the Improv, they got a call from a casting director that was doing *Police Academy 4*. (The good one.) They were looking for a wisecracking skateboarding kid and they had been in the audience a week before and seen me perform. This was the best thing about the Improv. There was always someone in the crowd who could help you—a director, a casting director, an actor, a famous comedian, studio executive, or just a friend of any of those people who would tell them about you. So I went in for the "audition," and the casting director told me there was no script. Those of you who have seen this movie can surely believe that this is true. My character was a new addition, and they were actually waiting for a new draft of the script. BUT THANK GOD THEY DIDN'T HAVE ONE, because I haven't mentioned this yet but I had no idea HOW TO FUCKING ACT! I'd never had a class, I'd never read a book about it, I thought it was overrated. I sort of figured myself to be some kind of "natural" like Eddie Murphy. They put me in front of a camera and told me to say some things about skateboarding that I might say to a cop, and use some skateboarding terms and just make up stuff. This was music to my ears. I'm pretty good on my feet at improvising and I had been skateboarding for ten years. So I talked about how I hurt myself during an *aerial axle stall* and fell from the *coping to the drain* broke my wrist. I threw in some jokes. They asked a lot of questions, but thank God none of the questions were "Do you know how the fuck to act dude?" since I can promise you I never would have gotten that part if I had to answer that.

Reading an audition off a script, I found out later, was unbelievably hard. We'll get to that later. So I ship off to Toronto in shock that I have a role in a movie series I've actually heard of, starring the Goot! (Steve Guttenberg). I get to my hotel and only two of us from the cast are at this particular establishment—me and none other than Sharon Stone. Sharon was drop-dead gorgeous (of course) and a total sweetheart to me. She wasn't a huge star yet (obv) or she would not have been anywhere near this movie. I quietly stared at her night and day throughout shooting, which was one very nice perk of working on the movie. Money was also a nice perk. I made $2,500 a week for ten weeks. "Run of the picture," they call it. I was flying high.

I got to do my own skateboarding and show off for all the ladies on set, which was a blast. I had to have a stunt double for the hard skateboarding stuff so they brought in pro boarders from the "Bones Brigade," on the west coast Chris Miller and Tony Hawk. Chris was closer to my size and look but rode regular foot. Tony was two feet taller than me but he rode goofy foot and I rode goofy foot so that made a little more sense. (*Goofy foot* is term to describe which way your feet go on your skateboard. When you face forward on the board my toes point to the left; when you're regular foot, you point to the right. That's a fact you'll never need again in your life.)

Back to the cash. I had never made this much money before, so I actually felt "rich." I remember walking down Toronto's main street with $300 on me. I was looking in a window. Inside I see pants that were $60 which is a lot and I thought, I could just go in there and buy those pants. They would never think I had this much money. It was like *Pretty Woman* except they would probably have treated me like more of a whore.

The movies ended and I flew back to Los Angeles with $10,000 cash on me, like a regular old Floyd Mayweather. I considered stopping at a strip club and making it rain/downpour. I could have pulled a Chris Brown and really had fun for an hour and a half. But no, I decided I was going to be smart about this. I gave my mom $3,000. God knows I owed her that and more. I paid for my bills, and I had 6K left to buy a car.

Now, buying a car is fun. I had never had anywhere near six thousand dollars to plunk down on wheels. This much money was enough to get me a car better than my last two cars put together, which had cost me $300 and $1,000 respectively. So I pored through *Auto Trader* (like Joe Dirt looking for a Hemi) and started to get weak hanging on to the Camaro page for too long. I was dog-earing cars that I should not have been looking at. I needed a basic, reliable, gas-efficient, boring car—not some tricked-out muscle car. So, going against my urge to buy a sweet pussy wagon like Greased Lightnin', I decided on a boring, dark gray, two-door Honda Accord hatchback. It had good gas mileage and that's about it. I did spring for the sunroof to make it a bit more of a pimp sled. And it was exactly $6,000 bucks. I called some woman met her down at Factor's Deli on Pico. I walked around the car, tire-kicked it a bit like I knew what I was doing . . . had her pop the hood . . . engine was in there, check. We were on the right track. I then bust out an envelope with sixty crisp hundred-dollar bills, forked it over, shook hands and left.

I was now a proud owner of a Honda. I headed off to the Improv high as a kite, with a new car I just bought with money from a movie

I just made. Now I had a spot at the world-famous Improv. I had the L.A. thing down. After my set, I invited Tim Rose, who had also been on that night, to come out and check out my badass car, like he would be so amazed to see an '83 Accord. But he was cool. As we were walking down the street, Tim started getting antsy, because we'd already been strolling for four or five minutes and no car. Then it dawned on me that my car was gone. It had been towed. Holy Crap. I did the walk of shame back to the Improv and got on the pay phone. (Yes, folks, a pay phone. I know they are gross. In fact I think that's how I got crabs five times in high school.) Anyway. The tow yard then informed me my car was not there.

Holy fuck. It got stolen.

I turned white. I'm already white. I got whiter.

I'd had this goddamn car for not even an hour, and now it was gone. I had no insurance. I never even put it in reverse! I just sat there, staring into space, thinking, I just shot a movie for ten weeks and I'm exactly where I was the day before I left. I have no money. And no car. I was embarrassed. And I was pissed off.

I slinked off into the night, sadly walking all the way back to my shitty futon in my shitty sublet apartment in the gay neighborhood that I didn't know was gay. A few tears might have been squeaked out along the way. I know all of you think of me as a tough guy, a hardass, an athlete in movies and TV, but this one got to me, folks. As if this town weren't hard enough, it took my car just to bitch-slap me for having a few minutes when I felt things were going the right way. I had never gotten so much nothing for $6,000 dollars. I would have been better off running on the 405 freeway at noon, naked, throwing all sixty hundred-dollar bills in the air. At least I would have gotten some press out of it.

CHAPTER SEVEN
LOSING MY HEAT

So what next? I was still broke. Running low on Top Ramen. With my pride empty, I went to see Bobcat Goldthwait. He was always nice to me and now I was there to abuse the friendship. I couldn't ask the Funny Boys for more; they had already done enough. It was Bob's turn to take on the burden of Spade. (Side note: There was this guy, Tim Rose, who I knew growing up in Arizona. He has a rich older brother, and right when I started doing stand-up in Arizona I made Tim's brother this offer, even though I didn't know him well . . . I told him that if he would cover a tiny apartment in L.A. and buy me a crappy car, he could have 15 percent of whatever I made for my whole career. I said I'd sign whatever he wanted. He didn't take me up on this unbelievable deal. But he did call about five years ago and said he'd thought it over and he'd roll the dice with me now, and asked me what kind of shitty car I wanted.) By the way, most of you already know this but it's very, very embarrassing to ask friends for money, even if it's legit, and I've done it a lot. That's why when people do it to me now I try to make it easier for them because I know how horrifying it is. I usually just say "strip first" or whatever. Dana Carvey once told me he gets nickel-and-dimed so much by acquaintances and so-called friends that sometimes it's worth the eight hundred bucks just to never talk to them again. Because if they aren't a close friend you know for sure they are not paying you back, so they avoid you forever once you give them the cash. Sounds harsh but for some shady people, it's a good idea. Chris Rock also told me that when I started to get money, be careful because most people highball you. He always says he gives half of the amount they ask for because he knows they pad it with extra shit like a new surfboard or some drug money. So if they ask for ten grand, he gives them five. It's not a bad system. But I usually give full freight because I feel too condescending asking what they "really" need it for. It's not my business. Chris also says, "You ever lend people money and they have the balls to buy shit in front of you? Dude, don't you owe me eight hundred bucks? You're buying a coat?" Chris is funny and I like him better now that I can use his jokes in my book and the laugh sort of counts on my stats. Sweet.

Anyway, now I was back to square one. But I had a movie under my belt, which was great. It gave me some "heat," as they say in the biz. Which is what you need to jump-start things. So right before I left I signed with a respected agent. I had gotten a manager, Marc Gurvitz who worked at Brillstein, right before I got the movie, too. He had seen me at the Improv. So they made my *Police Academy* deal and now aside from my screwup with the stolen car I was back on track. I wound up borrowing another six grand from Bobcat. This was very tough to go in for a reload but he said he wasn't worried because I would work a lot. Very nice guy and very cool of him. I signed a note saying I'd give it back in a year. It seemed feasible. So now I went to buy another car so I can hit the audition world. But what do I get? Dark gray '83 Honda Accord. The exact same car. But this time four-door, which I liked better. Weird how I found almost the exact same car but this time I insured it first. By the way, I told the police the woman who sold it to me originally probably had someone follow me with a duplicate key and just stole it back. He agreed, and then proceeded not to give a shit and do nothing about it.

So now I had a car and I was staying at that studio apartment and ready to party. My manager then informed me that my agent had left a big agency (no names: lawsuit alert) I already took it out and gone off on her own. So, I'm like, What the fuck? I liked her, what do I do? He said the big agency still wanted me and we should stay there. So they assigned me another agent. Now this is a tough replacement, because it wasn't someone who had gone out loved me and fought to get me. This was a person saying, "Sure, I'll look after them in case they hit it big." But the agent had no real stake in my career. And they might have even thought that I sucked. But still I thought I was in great hands Cause it was what? A big agency.

Our first call was to Steve Holland, a director Bob introduced me to up in Toronto who had me read parts of his script to him as sort of an impromptu audition up there. He said he was still interested in me for the lead in a new Fox pilot called *Beans Baxter*. I guess that's what I read scenes from. Fox was still sort of a newer network and didn't have tons of respect at the time. But we all know that it turned out to be a monster. So because I have good agency and manager and a little "heat" they somehow get this guy to offer me the part without ever going back in to audition again. This is a miracle. I'd never *really* acted, still never taken a class; I just got lucky. Because I got a good response in my month or two at the Improv and a movie. People thought I was about to blow up and needed to jump on it. So guess what?

We turned down the part.

This was *crazy* to me. I hadn't gone on one audition and they want to turn down a straight-up offer? I always wanted to be on a half-hour comedy this seemed like a perfect fit. It was about an FBI agent who's undercover as a high school kid or something. I loved it. I went in to the big agency and all these agents came together in a room to meet me.

"I think you're too good for this. Fox isn't big enough. You have heat. We are setting you up to meet NBC, ABC, and CBS. That's where you should be." This is what they told me. I'm like, "Well, I haven't really done jack shit. I mean, isn't this huge? My own fucking show? I can't picture why I would say no." I don't get it.

"Trust us, you're going to get a show on one of the big three."

So I trusted them. I went against all gut feeling and said, "I guess you guys know what you're doing. I'm new to this." I also fell victim to believing the hype.

Now I had to go on meetings with all the networks because pilot season was hitting. So here I was, the guy in the '83 Accord, bopping around audition for every show in town. *And being horrible at it*. I had no idea how to act. Literally. I would just stare at pages, always sitting, read stage directions out loud, etc. etc. etc. Such a goddamn rookie. But I didn't care because I knew they would see through all this bumbling and hire me because I was a "natural" and I had . . . "heat." Over two months I had about thirty auditions I got the same feedback every time: "He sucks. He's too green." That's a way of saying I'm shitty at auditioning, I have no experience, and no amount of heat and hype was going to get me hired. I basically burned every bridge to every casting agent and network exec in town. I came out the other side of pilot season with nothing but a bad rep and no show. The only thing I got was reading in *Variety* that *Beans Baxter* was a great pilot and Fox was going to make it a series. Without me! I couldn't have felt sicker. What a huge fuckup. I had exactly what I wanted and got talked out of it. I made a vow to always stick with my gut feeling and speak my mind. I swore this would never happen again. (It has happened about um five hundred thousand times since then. But, I'm a pussy.) So what do you want.

My manager Marc now had a game plan to shake shit up. He knew I was on the ropes and about to jump off a ledge. He told me I should leave this big agency. Fuck them. They hadn't helped me enough and they gave me bad advice. He knew a midlevel agent somewhere else who was great and thinks I'm hilarious. And would love to represent me. So with my head spinning, knowing I had turned down a great job and that the whole town knew I was a fraud, I agreed. Plus, more bad news: all my precious heat was officially gone. I was in worse shape than when I got to town. This was crushing me. I went from zero to a hundred back to zero. Frozen.

Now I signed up for an acting class way late. It finally was time. I was back to square one but at least I had an agent (that liked me) and a great manager. So these classes were crucial. Every casting director I met with would not see me again because I was so bad. I had to get some classes under my belt and try to get back in to see them again and change their minds. This was quite a job. So I signed up with the great Roy London, but his class is overflowing so I take his protégé, Ivana Chubbuck. Now she was a blast. A bit kooky but very good. I took the class two times a week and I would do stand-up in town or on the road the other times. I was getting serious about this shit. I couldn't float by on my "charm" and "natural ability." By the way, class was way harder than I thought too. My buddy Rob Schneider, whom I met doing stand-up, took them with me. So did Julie Warner, who ended up in *Tommy Boy* years later. We all had fun in class and it was like school. Lots of meeting with flaky scene partners and getting props and studying lines . . . etc. You would do about one scene a week and you had to be ready. Because if not you would be ripped apart in front of the whole class. Even worse, half the class consisted of babes who had just moved to L.A. to act, so when you were bad they were like, "I might have fucked this guy but now it's confirmed by the teacher that he's a talentless piece of shit I'll just go nail Piven." But even with all these ups and downs I have to say these classes really helped me. They gave me a better understanding of how to break down a scene and how to audition and a million other intangibles and definitely confidence.

Every few days the Improv would have some important person in the crowd. It was a gift to go onstage there. Auditions were basically coming to you. On top of that they had a lot of showcases. That's when a casting agent or director wanted to see a bunch of comedians for a specific show or movie part. One night the guy who books Johnny Carson would be in, a week later *Star Search* guy, a day later someone looking for a funny friend of the lead actor in a movie . . . etc. . . . But just to get *on* those showcases was very hard. You had to beg and call and hang around and hope somebody saw you and called you to put you on the list of people they wanted to see. I weaseled on a few of these and one day got a call from a scout for the Joan Rivers's show. He said they wanted to book me as a stand-up. Wow now, when Joan started, this was a huge deal. She turned her back on Carson (as the story goes) and she was competing against him now in late night. I was miles away from getting on Carson but this was somewhat in my vicinity. My manager told me one day that I got the booking. As I was shitting and celebrating he said, "Oh, by the way, *Star Search* wants you, too, but we can't do both." Cause there's a conflict.

I was like, "Okay, cool, cool." I said that very quickly but down deep I was wondering if I'd rather do *Star Search*. I had auditioned for *Star Search* in Arizona at a mall two years earlier and never got a callback. So embarrassing. Standing near a fountain below Chess King ripping through my two minutes allowed. But being new and in a small town, you'll do whatever. It was like in later years having *American Idol* come to your town. When you don't have money to travel, this is the thing you have to try. So I tried. And whiffed. But now I get to turn them down. Huge victory or shoulder shrugger? Turns out they survived without me. (Answer was shoulder shrugger.)

Now I finally got to do my first TV stand-up. And it was on Joan Rivers's newish talk show. I was of course scared shitless. I had my Guess brown button-down shirt with pearl buttons all laid out. This was the shirt I was sure I "looked good" in. I had no confirmation of this but was going by hunch (and mirror).

I got a call right before it that there was going to be a guest host that week. Joan was taking a vacation. (She was probably aware that the show was tanking and her vacation was meetings to plot her next move.) I was told that of course I would still go on; I really had no say in the matter. I was happy to know the guest host would be a comedian I had heard of named Arsenio Hall. So I prepped my set and brought my roommate down and pretty much crushed it. Bits went well, but one thing that stuck with me was I sort of blacked out in the middle, or I should say blanked out. One word in my act didn't come to me right away and I quickly replaced it with a similar word. But that really got to me. It probably wasn't noticeable but to me, it was a huge fuckup. I had done those bits a hundred times—how in the fuck could I blank? I have to chalk it up to the nerves of playing live TV. When you see a comedian on TV he's standing in front of a curtain and looking great and you hear a polite crowd. That's what I was used to! But when you *perform* on a talk show it's totally different. You walk out and see the flip side. Brighter lights than I've even been in, like a police interrogation, that's the first thing I wasn't ready for. Then the crowd; all I could think was, Wow, it's smaller in here than it seems on TV, and they are so far away. Oh look, that guy has a Hawaiian shirt oh he's wearing shorts inside. THESE WERE MY THOUGHTS FOLKS, NOT MY ACT! And there were four cameras with chubby bored cameramen behind me. "I wonder how much that guy makes?" THIS WAS IN MY BRAIN INSTEAD OF MY JOKES! This is what's called being spooked. It's like a horse. It wasn't what I was used to and I had to get my brain back on track in my five-second walk to my mark, which was a black X on the ground.

Wow, the stage is so shiny and polished . . . MORE SHIT UNFOCUSING ME. DO YOUR GODDAMNED ACT, SPADE.

Luckily the show got a good reaction. My manager and agent were getting calls again. Nothing like before, but a few curiosity calls. Fine. This was good because I'd been trying to dethaw for months. Trying to get a smithereen of heat again. Two weeks later I was in Salt Lake City playing Cartoons (most clubs have dumb names) and I got a call from my manager. They wanted me back on Joan. But not to do stand-up—to guest host! FOLKS WTF? I didn't get it, I had never even done a TV show before, that was my first one. How would I ever be able to host? But there was trouble at Joan's show and they were sort of auditioning people to take over. I really didn't understand all that but I was floored they thought I could handle it and be good at it. I had just turned twenty-three that week. I ultimately passed on hosting for a night, which shocked everyone. I just felt like I did my best set a week before and if I did anything less or looked nervous I'd be dismissed and thrown in the scrap heap. I couldn't erase any potential heat I had without thinking it through. So I passed mostly out of fear. This perked up the ears of Fox executives, so they called me in for a meeting. I got to sit down with Garth Ancier and Barry Diller. Barry was the big boss and Garth was the new president. It went well. They said they were curious as to why I turned down something so big so early in my career. I said I didn't want to fuck it up and I wasn't ready for that yet, and that ultimately I wanted to be on a sitcom. They respected that and said they would keep an eye out for me. So now I was finally starting to inch back into the town's good graces.

Every year HBO had a showcase to look for comics to appear in the annual *Young Comedians Special*. Getting onto that show was a huge deal for me, and a huge deal in general. This was the show that broke Sam Kinison, among many others. A slot on that show meant millions of people will know you.

Landing the HBO *Young Comedians Special* would be just the right thing to get me "hot" again. I knew it. *Hot* is a gross term used in Hollywood that I never say but it seems to make sense to people so I'm using it.

Even getting on the HBO showcase at the Improv to be seen was hard, but I squeaked through. The first year I didn't make it from the showcase onto the special. It killed me. They said I was good but wasn't ready, blah-blah. I was pissed, because I now had to wait another full year to try out again. I went back to the club scene, taking small television and movie scraps whenever I could get them. It's so funny now to look back and see what could have been. During this time I got very close on two very different shows, *In the Heat of the Night* and *Full House*. For *Full House* I had several callbacks for Joey's part, the role that eventually went to Dave

Coulier. I remember the audition had some bit about socks and I had that fucker memorized. But in the end I didn't get that part and I was so crushed because I felt I was letting everyone down, especially my mom, because back home there was a lot of mumbling and grumbling about my career not taking off and it was tough for me to hear and it was tough for my Mom to listen to.

This stress was killing me. I was getting vertigo, which was probably from grinding teeth, which was from this town killing me. It happens to almost everyone. You think you can handle it and you're ready for anything, like the parking tickets, the traffic, the no friends, but theres intangibles that get to you. The way people dismiss you when you do a bad audition, the time it takes for your agent to call you back. It's sort of slow death (and I sound so dramatic, but that's only because I'm a pussy). On a cheerier note, I had a great audition for *In the Heat of the Night*, which was surprising to everyone because this was a drama. This was serious. I had to play a southern police deputy opposite Carroll O'Connor, who was a mega TV star. For some reason, I nailed it. I was so happy. I got a callback. Then another one. Then another one. I was this close to getting this part, only to lose it at the last minute. Looking back I realize everything happened for a reason, but you could not tell me that then.

I kept getting crushed by these close calls. But I would have been on either of these shows for seven years and my whole life would have been different. If I had landed *In the Heat of the Night*, I would have been stuck in sweaty New Orleans for seven years with my nuts glued to my legs and no time for comedy. Back then, I just had tunnel vision to get the gig. Now I think of how lucky I am that neither of these happened.

So another half-assed year went by and here comes the HBO *Young Comedians Special* showcase again. And I whiff. They pass on me again. But for some reason, the slots go to already estab-

lished comics at the time, like Richard Belzer. WTF, HBO? I'm
ACTUALLY A YOUNG COMEDIAN, FOLKS! This was another near death blow, so I tuck my tail between my legs where
it felt most comfortable and headed back to bit parts on *Alf* and
Baywatch. (One of those was more fun than the other. You decide.)

I also head back on the road, which by this point had become
my life. Dallas, Cleveland, San Diego, New York . . . some were
great, some truly sucked. But New York was by far the toughest.
I had a buddy who was attending Columbia back then, so when I
"wanted" to work the New York comedy circuit (I use quotes here
around "wanted" because I didn't want to take these trips at all, as
you will see; this comedy circuit was more like a trip to the hole)
I had to call my friend and ask if I could crash there. I also had to
call this dude Gary Grant (who was like a booking agent). I don't
even think I ever met him, but he was tapped into tons of random
comedy gigs around New York and Jersey. Mostly the gigs were
just stupid one-nighters for seventy-five bucks a pop. Once I called
Gary, the production began. I had to fly to New York, which was
expensive. Then I would stay with my buddy at Columbia. The only
place he had room for me to sleep was sideways on a love seat, with
my feet on an ottoman. (Great for the bad neck, folks! There's a
reason you don't see this position in a mattress commercial.) I did
this for a month and I was creaky and stiff as hell. But if I had to
pay for a room, the paltry earnings I received from gigging would
have disappeared.

When I did have a show this was the basic drill: I would suit
up in my lame "New York" coat. (Being from Arizona, I really
didn't have a heavy coat, so I bought a wool herringbone coat from
a thrift store. It was referred to from then on as my "New York"
coat and yes, it looked stupid on me.) Then I'd drag my mom's
small honeymoon suitcase of props down to the subway. (This was

a feminine light blue suitcase from my mom's honeymoon with her initials on it.) It was sort of a "please mug me and/or rape me" look. If anyone's curious about the contents of my light blue "prop suitcase," one of the props was a small toy xylophone from my killer *Jeopardy!* bit, which was super-reliable and a possible closer. Very solid bit. I also had a cardboard thing for a dynamite *Wheel of Fortune* bit (mixed results), and most cringy, I carried my Tom Petty hat, which I stole off a valet parker at a New Orleans hotel for my big Petty impression. It was all so embarrassing.

I would take the subway in the cold down to Forty-Second Street, walk another half mile to the Improv, wait for some New York comedian with a car who was going to drive us to a gig outside the city. These one-nighters were between thirty minutes and two hours away. The guy who took me the first night I did all this was thirty-six years old. I remember thinking, *Holy shit this guy's old. If I'm still doing this at thirty-six times four please blow my brains out. Because that's inching up on me.*

Once one of these dogshit gigs was eight hours away, in Watertown, New York. This meant that I had to stay overnight. I clearly wanted to be a comedian so badly that I was willing to drive with a total stranger, for eight hours in his Nova, to a tiny town, making shitty small talk, for a shitty show, to stay in a shitty hotel, to shove off again the next morning. It was life on a hamster wheel, but it was what you had to do. There were no apps to see if this guy was a registered sex offender. This was the Old West (in the East).

One time when I got back to the Improv after one of these trips, two comics there asked me if I wanted to go smoke crack with them. I politely declined. Then they said, "You got seventy-five bucks tonight, what are you going to do with it?" I said, "Blow eight dollars on a cab to my friend's place, use some for food maybe, and save a bit." They laughed and one of them said, mostly to his buddy, "If I ever wake up the day after a gig and there's money in my pocket I know I did something wrong." They both cracked up at this. I'm not sure why I remember that exchange so vividly, but it stuck with me. Those guys were just doing gigs to tread water. And buy crack, I guess. I wanted a life out of it.

The roughest thing about those New York trips was that I lived like a grimy little roof rat but still barely came out ahead. After a solid month back east, I would fly home to L.A. and only clear five hundred dollars. The experience was valuable, but man it was a lot of shit to eat for five hundo. Six months after I was home, I'd realize I had to do it again. Running low on funds and scraping by. My two twenty-eight-dollar spots at the L.A. Improv a week, and zero movie parts, weren't exactly paying the bills.

One night I was hanging in the hallway of the Improv on L.A.'s Melrose Avenue dreading my flight the next day to depressing New York and who walks by but Budd Friedman. Budd was owner of the Improv and biggest cheese at the club. He could make or break you, basically. He could put you in showcases, give you great spots, or cut you out. Luckily, he was always very kind to me. He let me host at the Improv all the time, which to be honest was tedious because it meant that I only got to do a five-minute set at the top, and then had to wait by the stage door to introduce every act for the rest of the night, but it was a gift to just be in the mix, to meet and see tons of great comics. I developed a sense of who I liked and who I didn't, and my style was sort of a research paper of all my favorites. Dennis Miller, Kevin Nealon, Steven Wright, they became my subjects. I liked the subtle throwaway jokes, and I gravitated toward that style and kept it.

That night, Budd stopped me in the hall and said, "Hello, David. Did you know we opened an Improv in Las Vegas at the Riviera?" I said, "No, I did not." He said, "Do you want to play it this week? You'd have to leave tomorrow, but it's five hundred dollars for seven days." HOLY SHIT! Five hundred is what I clear after a month of shit gigs in crummy Jersey with thirty-five-year-old crackhead comics. Yes, of course I want to go to sunny, juicy Vegas, which reminds me of Arizona! But I just nodded, "Sure, sounds like fun," even though I was totally stoked but that hallway was too tight for cartwheels. Five hundred dollars, here I come!

I canceled my New York trip and hopped in my car the next day heading for Lost Wages (I mean Las Vegas, lolololol). It's a bleak drive but I didn't care, I was playing the Strip! It's a six-hour drive through the desert and you pass the strangest things along the way. There's not much happening on that stretch of highway except a clump of fast-food places every fifty miles and maybe a random 99-cent store in case you need some yarn or thumbtacks.

So I got to my exciting Riviera gig. It's summer so I was frying but I didn't give a fuck. I'm a tough dude from the mean streets of Scottsdale, Arizona. I found out that I was opening for Jackie Vernon, who is sort of a comedy legend, or if not a legend at least well-known. (This was the status I was shooting for. Legend seemed a bit out of reach.) My name was on the marquee. A smarter kid would have taken a picture, but I didn't, so I can't show you. (It's not like today, where I would have thirty pictures of my walk to the marquee and a Snapchat of me staring at it and narrating.)

The deal at the Improv was that everybody did a short set. On a regular road gig, let's say the Dallas Improv, there is an MC/opener who opens the show and does about ten minutes, then a middle/feature act who goes on and does twenty-five to thirty minutes, and then the headliner, who does forty-five minutes to an hour. At the Riviera Improv it was scaled down. I was the

MC, so I did six minutes up front, then I bring another guy to do eight, and another better guy does twelve, and the headliner does twenty-five. And we did this show THREE TIMES A NIGHT! THAT'S TWENTY-ONE SHOWS A WEEK, FOLKS! It was sort of brutal because as the MC, I had to be around for everything again. I couldn't really drift off because I might miss bringing up the next guy. It was fucking tedious but way better than my little blue suitcase and guys pushing thirty-seven in New York. I hung backstage with Steve Schirripa, who was the doorman at the Riv. He's the big Italian guy who later went on to star on *The Sopranos* as Bobby. He was such a classic Vegas goombah. He told me when I got there to be on time, not fuck around, and keep my sets tight. One night I drifted off into the casino (classic) during someone's set, and came back one minute late. ONE MINUTE FOLKS! So the eight-minute guy had to bring on the twelve-minute guy. Oh BOO HOO. I didn't think it was a big deal but Schirripa was pissed. He told me to leave! I had to go back to my room and "think about what I did." Like I was a kid. So stupid. "Who cares, I'll just bring up the headliner." "No, you fucked up, you get out of here." What a walk of shame back to my room that was.

To add insult to inj (abbreviated), the comics didn't even get to stay at the Riv; we had to stay at the shithouse dogshit La Conchaka or some other oddly named ghetto motel next door, there were only six floors in it and each had its own color. Like six floors and every room was a color. I stayed on red the first time. I got gold the next. So weird. Anyway, I slinked back to my dumb red room and I was scared shitless Steve was going to rat me out to Budd and I'd get fired. My whole life I worried about getting fired. I was worried about it during all my busboy and dishwasher jobs. (I did get fired from those.) I was always stressed at road gigs when I wasn't killing (once got fired for that) and always felt the heat during the first five years of *Saturday Night Live*. Just always, always, always! (No relation to "Marcia, Marcia, Marcia!") No wonder my neck is tight.

But mostly during the Vegas week I was in heaven. One day I snuck over to do some tanning (I know it's so girlie, but I admit it) at the Riviera pool. I grabbed a towel and a chair and cranked my Walkman. That was the only "rich" thing I had. I would hold it up for the ladies to see and get horny about. For food I was obviously on a snug budget, but luckily the Improv gave me twenty-one coupons for twenty-one meals at the Riviera employee cafeteria that week. It was a dump but I was always in there. The only bummer was that my dates didn't see the "charm" in the place; I'd say "keep quiet and ask Hector the bellman if you can finish his omelet." On a side note, the comic I worked with the first time at the Riviera had weird hair. Now, I know I have weird hair but this was different. We all thought it was clearly a toupee but he was like twenty-eight and had longish brown hair, so we weren't sure. But then on Wednesday he came to the show with short hair? He casually mentioned he got a haircut. So wig rumors dissipated . . . UNTIL YEARS LATER when I found out this was his trick! He had two toupees. One long, and one short! He would switch it every week on Wednesday and say he got a haircut. WHAT A GREAT MOVE! GENIUS. I had mad respect for that fucking scam. I was fully hoodwinked.

It was hard not to hit the casino and blow all my piddly earnings, I have to admit. You have so much free time on the road, and besides that, to get to the Improv stage I had to walk through the whole casino, which was so fucking tempting. Slots, roulette, blackjack, and even baccarat, which I still don't understand, they were five feet away at all times. Every day was a real lesson in restraint. The showroom was right next to Foxy Boxing, which was also tempting. Never nailed a foxy boxer. Still mad about that.

When the week was over, the Riv asked me if I wanted to be paid in chips. Are you kidding me?? Do I look like a moron?! I took the check and I hightailed it, thinking that this was the easiest five hundo I had made in a *loooong* time. I hung on to that fucking thing for dear life all the way home to L.A.

CHAPTER EIGHT

HBO *YOUNG COMEDIANS SPECIAL*

It was 1989 and I was still kicking around the Improv, averaging two weeks on the road and two weeks in town trying to get auditions and doing spots. My third attempt to get on to the HBO *Young Comedians Special* was around the corner. This time I had a foot in the door because Brillstein-Grey was producing the show that year, and Brad Grey is one of my managers, along with Marc Gurvitz. I felt like this gave me a great shot at getting on. When the showcase came around, I knew they were looking for five comics. You forget that they are also looking in Chicago, New York, all over the country—not just Los Angeles. This special was still a huge deal in a world with four networks and barely any cable channels. Even with what I viewed as a leg up, I was sweating it. When the showcase came around, I decided not to do the set I had done the previous two years. I felt I couldn't repeat it. It didn't work twice anyway so this seemed like a no-brainer, but a tight set is a security blanket. (It usually is pretty foolproof.) When you're a comedian, you create a set and you know it works and you sometimes find yourself going back to it. It just happens. You have your go-to six-minute set, your ten-minute set, thirty, etc. For the showcase, the producers usually wanted to see six minutes. I knew I had to shake it up. Even if I had a great thirty-minute set, the six minutes I audition with have to be even better than great, so it is hard to take a risk and gamble with material that isn't tried and true. This all may sound stupid, but that's all we comedians think about.

The night came around and when I did my set and I felt pretty good about it, even though I had stepped outside of my comfort zone. I did a newer bit about doctors recommending Nuprin for pain over Vicodin and threw in my Michael J. Fox impression. There are a lot of good comics in the showcase, though, and I knew I had to wait to hear my fate. This was not easy. I started calling my managers every day to get feedback (thirsty!) and at first I heard I had a spot in the special. I was over the moon. Days went by. I started to hear that though I did well, my managers were not sure if I made it or not. Now word gets around of some other guys who got slots. Now I started to shit my pants a bit. Was I getting passed over again? Dennis Miller was hosting that year and he was my favorite comic at the time. I even knew him a little bit, as he was also with Brillstein-Grey as a client. I felt like that was one more piece of the puzzle that should get me on. I should fall into the right-place-at-the-right-time category. Next comes word that HBO is passing. This hurls me into the beginnings of a deep depression.

I realize that my career is falling apart. I came out of the gate big with *Police Academy 4* ("big" is relative, okay) and then turned down a Fox pilot. (It got canceled after two years, but only because I didn't star in it. I'm convinced.) My entire career and the possibility of ever getting laid again were riding on getting this HBO slot. I'm in the dumps. I hate showing my face back in Arizona, where half the people don't want me to do well because they are jealous, and the other half want someone from their city to put the town on the map. It was awful.

I finally got a call. "They liked you, but you are their sixth pick and they only have room for five." BUZZKILL! (Cue theme from *M*A*S*H:* "Suicide Is Painless.") The five who were chosen are Jann Karam, Fred Stoller, Warren Thomas, Rob Schneider, and Drake Sather. I didn't know how to take this news. Again I was good but not good enough.

Then Dennis Miller and Brad Grey started pushing HBO to use me in the show. They didn't want to kick someone else off—they just wanted to help me get my slot. Somehow they talked HBO into spotlighting six comedians instead of five. This was the first time that this had ever happened, and it had happened for me. We would all just do shorter sets. No prob! Major relief, actually! So I was on cloud eleven. Mom was happy. And the couple of a-holes back in Arizona who wanted me to fail could suck a dick.

The way HBO did the special was that they would pick a theater, pack it with comedy fans, and tape two shows in one night. Then they would cut those two shows together and use your best material, combined with shots of whichever was the best audience. All of the comics they had chosen were good, and I knew it would be hard to stand out. By the night of the taping I was shaking in my boots. It was like I was back at Arizona State, about to go on at Greek Sing. Actually I wasn't as freaked as I had been that night. I had Dennis Miller to help me relax this time. Plus, I had just done a weeklong guest stint on *Baywatch*, so my hair was extra blond and fluffy. I was feeling good about that. Unfortunately, I was also pretty sure I had contracted hep C because I had to go into the ocean for five minutes during shooting. I felt like that was enough time in the sewer to catch something gross. To add to my nerves, one of my all-time rock heroes, David Bowie, was in the audience that night. I don't know why he was there, but holy shit, Ziggy Stardust in the stands just made everything more terrifying.

I watched everyone else's set before I went on, and one thing shocked me. Warren Thomas wasn't that prepared. He went out and just started talking to the crowd, saying things like, "What else is going on?" It seemed like he was finding jokes as he went along. I asked him afterward why he had done that. He said, "I don't like to prepare it all perfectly. I usually let it flow when I'm at the clubs and see what happens. I'm good on my feet." I admired the balls of this, but it was something I never would have done or even considered. I had worked on my act for weeks, deciding which lines to say and when, and if something came out spontaneously, great, but I had my seven minutes ready to go. When my turn came, things went my way. The crowd was great to me. I had a strong set and when I saw the show air, they wound up using almost everything I did, which was a gift. I guess they trimmed Warren way back. He was a great comedian but that night the crowd was just not there for him and so he lost something very valuable: airtime on a national television show.

The HBO *Young Comedians Special* is the kind of thing that can land on the desk of someone like Lorne Michaels. It goes without saying that it is a game changer. A few weeks later, I got the call that some people at *Saturday Night Live* saw my set. My manager was at the Brillstein company, and the legendary Bernie Brillstein had handled *Saturday Night Live* talent his whole career . . . from John Belushi and Gilda Radner all the way to Lorne Michaels and many in between. Now, to be honest, I was always hoping to get on a sitcom and *SNL* wasn't even in my sights. I wasn't a character guy and it was also too way, way out of reach so I didn't bother thinking about it. Not that sitcoms were easy to get, but I could picture it more. But now I had a chance and I had better get mentally ready. You basically got one shot with them. Now was my time to strike. If I tanked, I wouldn't get a serious second look for a very long time. This was for real.

Both Rob Schneider and I got *SNL* auditions out of the HBO *Young Comedians Special*. Rob and I were super tight at this point. We had traveled in the same stand-up grooves for years, out in the Valley. We lived close to each other and hung out a lot. So, even though I had a friend in tow, I was still twenty-five and freaking out about flying to New York and having the biggest audition of my life. But a few weeks later, we took our first-class flights from LAX to JFK and were put up at the Omni Berkshire Hotel, a hotel I had actually heard of because . . . they always PLUG IT ON *SNL*. This was all quickly becoming too much for me. It was a beautiful hotel and we didn't even have to put our credit cards down when we got there, which was a good thing because I didn't have a credit card. But I was hungry so this created a bit of an issue. I didn't want to order food on my own dime, because it was so expensive. But I didn't want *Saturday Night Live* to hear that I charged dinner to them, because I didn't know if they were paying for it. And if they were paying for it, would they get mad that I had a club sandwich twice in one day? I kept warning Rob not to eat too much. He didn't seem to care at all. The whole time I was like, "Rob, that soup is eight bucks . . . don't get us fired before we're hired." (I hate that Lorne might read this book and realize Rob and I were drowning ourselves in soup and sandwiches and regret hiring us.)

The audition was scheduled at the famous Catch a Rising Star comedy club, where Rodney Dangerfield and many others started. I heard Michael Shoemaker and Marci Klein were coming to watch us. These were two of Lorne's right-hand men, even though Marci is a chick. Marci is Calvin Klein's daughter and played a big role in booking the hosts on the show. Michael Shoemaker seemed to be the number two under Lorne. This is what I was able to figure out just by asking around, trying to get some sense of what to expect with the audition. Most important, I knew that both had big votes in picking new cast members. I think Jim Downey, the head writer, was there that night as well. I found out later this was like jury duty to all these guys. They'd rather go to someone else's kid's soccer game. Dennis Miller even came as a show of support for Rob and me, which was very cool of him. Obviously we were both entirely panic-stricken at the notion of all these people in the audience. This was not a bullshit table read for *Alf*. This was *SNL*.

That night, there was another comic on after us, and the *SNL* troop was there to see him, too. Tom Kenny was very different from me. He was really funny and very high energy—in fact, he later wound up as the voice of SpongeBob SquarePants. He was a very cool guy, and I sort of got the impression that it was either going to go his way or mine that night. I went on first. We were each supposed to do fifteen to twenty minutes, and when I looked out into the room the first thing I noticed was that New York clubs were much smaller than I expected. I could never get spots like this when I came to the city in my dirty-couch/ottoman-surfing days. I could only get shitty one-nighters in the surrounding towns, so all of this was eye-opening for me. I also noticed that there were not many people in the room, and about 60 percent of them were from *SNL*. All of this is going through my head as I start dishing my A-level material and proceed to EAT IT.

Dennis Miller had given me a piece of advice a few days earlier that suddenly came to me. "When you audition, you don't want to kill too hard because that sends up a red flag. They'll think you're some polished road act." So by the time I get to my third joke, I think, Well, I sure am taking his advice! I sure as hell am not killing too hard. I got a few titters, but it was pretty much crickets my whole set. I didn't even do my full time. I think I left the stage after ten minutes, to try to stop the bleeding. Homemade tourniquet. Rob was next. Same situation. Rob had good jokes and he was a funny performer, but it was like the audience was scared to laugh at him. Rob exited the stage at around ten minutes, too. Cut to: Tom Kenny walks up and kills from beginning to end. I think he did his full set. It was like a fucking Arsenio audience howling at everything he said. Rob and I hung our heads and went back to the hotel and ordered soup.

The next night, Rob and I were back in the club. We were celebrating because we have gotten the call to be hired as writer/performers. Rob was so ecstatic. I was not. I said, "What are you talking about? I don't want to be a writer. I want to be on the show." He said, "Well, you start off as a writer like Chevy Chase did, like all those guys did. It's great news." I tried to be excited but honestly, I was just scared. I had no idea how to write a sketch. I barely knew how to write stand-up at this point. The scenario I had pictured if I somehow got on *SNL* involved their brilliant writers giving me funny things to do in sketches. I had no idea how hard the job I was about to get would be. But through that fear fog I finally shook myself and said, Holy fuck, I'm gonna be on *SNL*.

I flew back to Arizona and was chilling in my Motel 6 room when I got the official offer and terms of my job at *Saturday Night Live*. I was hired as a writer for the last four shows of the 1990 season, for $900 a week and a $1,500 bump if I happened to land in a sketch on the show. I remember writing all of this out on the Motel 6 stationery and hoping I would never have to stay at that Motel 6 again.

CHAPTER NINE
GETTING ON
SNL

t was mid-April of 1990 and I was flying out to *Saturday Night Live* to start my new job. It was a scary flight mostly because I'm scared of everything, but I was in first class, so that made it a little better. I'm such a first-class whore. After years of flying shitty Southwest flights for stand-up gigs, I couldn't believe that now I was getting the royal treatment, flying to my fancy new job in Rockefeller Center. It was back in the days where they had a curtain up between first and coach and the stewardess would make sure you couldn't even *see* the people in first class. She would tug that curtain shut and whisper a condescending "no peekinggggg" to the panhandlers in coach.

Now all I had to do was come up with ideas for funny sketches.

For the past five years, I had spent every waking moment—when I wasn't staring at girls or freaking about cash—coming up with jokes for my stand-up. But sketch is a completely different animal. I spent the whole flight going through all the characters I did in stand-up, deciding which ones I could put on the table as "my own" before I officially started writing sketches. When you work at *Saturday Night Live*, you get one free swing when you start to tell them the characters you have and want to own, because the second you walk into the writers' room, they own everything you come up with from that moment on. This is how it was when I was at *SNL*, anyway. It may have changed since then, but as I've already shared, my strongest characters involved a weak Tom Petty impression with a stolen valet hat. It isn't my strong suit.

So, on this plane trip, I didn't have a ton of great ideas, though I felt like this was my golden opportunity to claim an Opera Man or Wayne and Garth or something that might hit big. Skateboard Pizza guy . . . Drunk Astronaut . . . I was grasping at straws, just trying to get something down on paper. When we landed, I headed right for the Omni Berkshire, where they had the great soup and expensive room service. There's nothing better than having everything paid for. All my life I had been counting nickels, wearing crappy clothes, pushing my car when it ran out of gas. And here I was, living in a hotel for four weeks, for free, after my first-class flight. All I had to do was write something funny, or else this shit would end really quickly.

The first night after I arrived happened to be a Saturday, and Rob and I were invited to come see the show before we officially started working on it. Hanging out backstage was really exciting but it was also overwhelming and chaotic. I had no idea how I would fit in. I knew Dana Carvey and Kevin Nealon from staying at their houses when I was coming up, and of course Dennis Miller was there, so it wasn't like it was a sea of new faces. But everyone was running around busy, with a lot on their minds. I met a few other cast members on the fly and a few writers. I remember talking to Jon Lovitz for a few minutes. He seemed depressed so I asked him what was wrong. He said, "I am just kind of bummed. I'm only in two things this week." I was taken aback. "Wow, that's crazy," I said. "I would never think you guys count sketches. I just think you're funny and I'm glad when I see you." He said, "Yeah, well, Dana is in five things." That surprised me. I told myself to remember that conversation, because I never wanted to feel like that. Lovitz was such a big star to me and had such a great job, I couldn't believe he felt bad about having a light week on the show. Later I would learn just how hard it was to avoid obsessing over those very details.

On Monday, Rob and I went down to work together. I wanted to get there at noon, because I didn't want anyone saying I was late. Of course, no one gets there before one, which is one of the pluses of working at *SNL*. The problem is that I'm not a late-night person, and regardless of when I hit the hay I'm getting up at 9 A.M. Staying up all night was the worst part for me, but everyone else on staff totally got off on that. It was total crickets at the office until around 4 P.M., when the important people started to trickle in. I met Jim Downey, the head writer on the show, who was very cool but always had a ton of work on his plate and so didn't have time to baby the new guys like me. Rob and I were escorted to a tiny room and told, "Here's a wooden desk and a chair, and this is your office." There were no computers around back then, so we were told to write out our brilliant sketch ideas on yellow legal pads and then give them to one of four assistants whenever we needed them typed up. (So *Mad Men,* right?) I met Conan O'Brien, Bob Odenkirk, and Robert Smigel . . . all as nice as they could be for as busy as they were. Eventually I started to meet the cast, and before I knew it, it was the Monday meeting with the host. The host that week was Corbin Bernsen from the then hit show *L.A. Law*. After that Monday meeting, everyone sort of drifted off to write sketches.

I had been told it was Corbin ahead of time, so I had a little jump-start on my sketch idea . . . and that would never happen again. I went back to my tiny office and started trying to write sketches. My first sketch was not for Corbin at all, because I could not think of a good idea for him. (See what I mean? Stand-up comedians only write for themselves. You don't know the other person's comedic rhythm, you only know yours. So it was a hard switch to make at first.) I wound up putting all my eggs in the Jan Hooks basket that week. I had an idea for a sketch about Life Alert, where Jan would play an old lady who was so lonely she kept calling Life Alert just to hang out with the paramedics. As the sketch went on, her reasons for calling would become more and more absurd. "Life Alert . . . I stuck my hand in the toaster, and it's on dark! HURRY!" Life Alert was a big commercial back then so it seemed timely.

That sketch was read fourth out of forty-three at the table read on Wednesday. I later learned that being read early was a good sign. Mike Shoemaker, one of the talent coordinators, would create the order of the sketches in read-through. It became clear to me later that the first ten in the read-through had the best shot of making it onto the show, because everyone was ears open, high energy at that point. The read-through room probably had fifty people packed in it from every department—all the writers, the cast, the host, and of course Lorne. Having the fourth sketch up in read-through was great in my first week. Not having the host in it was not. Having the host in the sketch is key. Sometimes the host will choose to drop out of a sketch if they feel they are in too many and replace themselves with a cast member, but really, the goal is to make the host look good, so you are better off writing sketches that include them if you want your sketch to go.

So, my sketch came up fourth, and as it was read I started

to sweat and freak out more than I thought I would. It is such a tense, hot, sweaty, intimidating room that your heart starts pounding long before your turn comes up. When you write a sketch you get to walk around before read-through and coach people on how you play their parts . . . even the host. It's a fun micro-power trip to give direction to the host, I have to be honest. But with more than forty sketches on every week, the coaching doesn't always sink in, and suddenly you hear the host reading your sketch with some unexplainable Irish accent and you realize you're dead in the water. It's a common practice for a host to want to "try" things as an actor with your characters. "I thought I'd play uh, a character gay." Sometimes it helps. Sometimes it really bombs.

But I was in the clear, because I had gone with a cast member for my sketch, and Jan Hooks is about as good as it gets. I was so desperate for her to really nail it, because I knew it was my first chance to score as a writer. When we finally get to the sketch, I'm drenched in sweat. All the other writers are secretly wanting it to die. Jan read and did a great job, and I got some laughs, and then it was on to the next one. Mine was actually decently written because I had so much time with it and it blended in nicely. No heads turning like, "Who wrote this piece of shit?" The new guy?! After about twenty-two more sketches there was a break.

The second half of the table read is rough. The sketches aren't as good, the host is usually getting tired, and you see Lorne start yawning, you can imagine it's a bit of the nail in the coffin for your sketch. After read-through, Lorne, Robert Smigel, Jim Downey, Al Franken, all head into Lorne's office and lock the door to make their decisions. They write every sketch's name on a large index card and put it up on a corkboard. The corkboard has the beats of the show written out. First there's the cold opening, then the monologue. (Which doesn't usually get written until Saturday, scaring the shit out of every *SNL* host. On a side note, it's a sneaky

way for a writer to get something on the show if you put a monologue in read-through. Because if it works, the higher-ups will be
relieved they don't have to worry about it that week and might even
help you punch it up—and you still get the credit! That's a bonus!
It took me a while to figure this out.) Because it usually took about
two hours for the bosses to pick the sketches, it became our rit-
ual to head down to Wally's & Joseph's, an old-school steakhouse
nearby, for dinner. That place had been there for ages, deep in the
Theater District and not far from the studio. My pals and I would
go sweat it out over our Caesar salad, hoping that our cards would
land on the right part of the corkboard that week.

The game starts with all the cards on one side of the corkboard,
and as the decisions are made, the cards get plugged into the show
in the places that seem right. Back in my time, that might have
meant a Wayne's World cold opening card followed by the monologue (always "to come"), then a sketch or two, followed by Weekend Update, a few more sketches, even cards for commercials. At
the very end of the show there is room for one more sketch, which
is known around the campus as the 5-to-1 sketch, because it airs at
five minutes to 1 A.M. Those are sometimes the most interesting on
the show because of the weirdest, and the riskiest; that is when the
show has the fewest viewers. So they can gamble.

That night, I was sitting at dinner obsessing over my Jan Hooks
Life Alert sketch, feeling like I had a decent shot of getting something on the air the first week. Dennis Miller had already told
me that Rob and I had four shows to prove we were good writers
and to get a sketch on air. If that didn't happen, chances were we
wouldn't be asked back. So that was rattling around my head, too,
as I walked back to the studio. We drifted around aimlessly until
we finally heard, "Okay, the door is open!" We all gathered around
the corkboard, ready to meet our fate. Lorne and the rest of the big
dogs had already skedaddled because they don't want to hear the

bitching (a tactic they used every week I was there). I sneaked in, looked up at the board, searching for my sketch. I started at the end of the show and worked toward the front. My heart sank. No sketch. But what I did notice is that it was pinned on the right next to the sketches near Weekend Update. When I asked what that meant, Shoemaker told me, "It's because they liked it and it almost got on. You can tell the ones that stayed on the left side were the sketches that weren't even considered. If it has been moved it means they thought about it, but yours got outvoted." Sometimes you are in the show for two solid hours, and then in the last minute before they open the door, a switch is made and you're out.

The worst thing is when you realize not only did you not get any sketches on, but you aren't *in* any sketches, either. In that case your week is basically over on Wednesday at 10 P.M. That was my fate my first week at *SNL*. I headed back to the Omni Berkshire knowing that now I only had three shows to prove myself. I was tired, beat up, and, frankly, scared. As I walked out I saw all the writers who had landed sketches, and they were excitedly talking to the set designers. It just sucked. The amazing thing about *Saturday Night Live* (and I rarely say "amazing," unlike L.A. girls who use it five times in every sentence, mostly to describe a salad) the show isn't even planned until Wednesday at 10 P.M., and the live show is seventy-two hours away. Also, once the sketches are chosen, the process for how the show unfolds is amazing. The writers immediately go into action talking to set designers, then to wardrobe to pick out clothes, then to the wig department to discuss hair and whether each character should wear a wig or should the cast use their real hair. It was way more work than I thought, with a million decisions to be made. It looked like fun, but I just kept walking, because I wasn't a part of any of it.

Thursday is rehearsal day for the cast on whichever set is ready, which usually means there's tape on the ground where the walls will be after the set designers are done building them. The writers spend Thursdays rewriting sketches. I was under the impression (because no one will actually tell you what to do at *SNL*, you have to figure this shit out on your own) that you only came to rewrite day if you had a sketch that got on. So I had planned to spend my Thursday night dining alone with a notepad, instead of in the mandatory fifteen-hour day in the writers' room. I was at the Omni, just about to leave for dinner solo because I had no friends outside of the show, when Rob Schneider and Jim Downey called me from the writers' room. "Where the fuck are you?" Since I was in the dark, I said, "I didn't get anything on, I'm just hanging out." Downey said, "Get up here. You have to be in these meetings and help with jokes." I was so pissed at Rob. He had known about this meeting for more than a week but never mentioned it. To be honest, it was the beginning of the friction between us. I had totally missed another meeting he was in, too, so I wondered why he didn't share that with me. So every Thursday from then on, I was in that goddamn, sweaty writers' room, which happened to be the same room where we had the read-throughs. Those Thursdays were torture, especially back then, when there was no Instagram to check every eight minutes. It was fifteen hours of trying to add jokes to someone else's sketch to make them score, and make them look good. It was very humbling and a tough adjustment for me. I had only ever written jokes for myself. Now I'm handing over one-liners to a host or a cast member because I was at the bottom of the totem pole. I just got used to it, but honestly it took me longer than it should have. Cause I'm kind of a dick.

The next host up was Alec Baldwin, who turned out to be one of the all-time great *SNL* hosts. This was his first time hosting, and the episode that earned him an Emmy nomination. I remember seeing him in that first Monday meeting. He had just come off of *The Hunt for Red October* and he had this jet-black, slick-backed hair, and he just looked like a stud. I thought, This dude's a movie star.

I met over a hundred hosts during my time on the show, and there were definitely moments when I thought, This person has no charisma, little to no talent, and nothing special about them. They are just really lucky. And then there were a handful where I just said to myself, This person is a fucking star. I didn't know what to expect from Baldwin, to be honest, but he was a very upbeat, very fun guy, and he gave all the writers respect, including myself. He could do tons of different voices and a lot of accents. He was and still is exactly what you want in an *SNL* host. Talented and up for anything. Those are the hosts that score the most on the show.

The show was very good that night. On a live show, you get one take. Usually, on an average *SNL*, you get one or two awesome sketches and then a bunch of C-pluses. Movie stars come into the show and they are used to multiple tries to get something nailed. It doesn't work that way on *SNL*. The worst is when a sketch is killing in rehearsals all week, but on Saturday, something trips and it falls apart. Maybe a cast member misses a cue because something happened in wardrobe, or the whole thing just starts wrong and then the cast spends the rest of the time trying to recapture the magic they had in rehearsals but it just isn't there. But Baldwin, he was great in every sketch. He made me see how it's supposed to be done. Meanwhile, this was the second show in a row where I didn't get anything on. And I was starting to feel like I was legitimately in over my head.

Andrew Dice Clay was the host for my third show. His episode was the one that got the most attention of the entire season, but the wrong kind. Clay was the biggest comedian in the country at that time. He had just sold out two nights at Madison Square Garden, which was a remarkable coincidence because I had just done a gig in the back room at T.G.I. Friday's . . . and it looked pretty full.

Dice had gained a reputation for being a homophobic, sexist pig. His career was peaking and everyone was after him. His exaggerated character always made me laugh, but some people took his act very seriously. One of those people was Nora Dunn, a longtime and very valuable cast member on *SNL*. Nora made it clear she would not perform with Dice, making a crazy situation even crazier. Dice had so much pressure on him, I could tell he was sort of freaking out. He had this buddy with him named Hot Tub Johnny West, who had long hair that I swear was a wig and who was a dead ringer for Steve Perry from Journey. I'm not sure what his job was other than being Dice's friend, but I have a lot of guys in my life who have that job now, so I didn't have a problem with it. I don't know why they called him Hot Tub. All I could think about was a lot of hair in the filter. Anyway, I could tell Dice was getting more tense as the week went on. As a comedian, I couldn't imagine hosting the show, let alone having every person in America watching and hoping you fuck it up. There were definitely a lot of folks out there who hated this guy. I would have killed to have appeared in a sketch in this show, but with no pull, there was no chance. There was no demand for me from the audience, the writers, or Lorne. Once again I was stuck punching up.

Dice got heckled by protesters during his monologue, and his big comeback was something along the lines of "This is the kind of guy that goes into a public bathroom to smell other people's crap." I don't recall the exact quote, but that was the sentiment. It wasn't a great comeback and that stumble set the whole show off on the wrong foot. It wasn't the worst show in my run, but with so many people watching, we needed a home run and we probably hit a double. We weren't helped by the fact that our musical guest that night was Julee Cruise and the Spanic Boys. I like to look back at the musical guests and see who blew up after the show and who disappeared. I feel like this week it might have been the latter.

The last show in my four-show trial run before summer hiatus was hosted by Candice Bergen. She was stunningly gorgeous and so sweet. In the Monday meeting, you all start out on the same footing. You are all just faces in the crowd to the host. The host is obliged to treat everyone equally because they don't know who is important and who is not. As the week went by, most hosts realized that I was pointless, but at that Monday meeting I got a little bit of eye contact and attention. That was fun. But, as per my usual course, I didn't get anything on that week. I had two shots—one was a sketch I had written with Rob, and one was a bit for Weekend Update. Unfortunately, Rob forgot to put my name on the sketch we wrote together, so when the read-through came along, it looked like I was only writing sketches that I could appear in. I looked like a selfish prick. So I went to Rob and asked him what happened. His response was, "You left at two A.M. I stayed all night. I was bleary when I handed that thing in." I had left at 2 A.M. because we finished at 2 A.M. I didn't need to walk around in my boxer shorts to show everyone how late I had stayed up all night writing. It was a little obvious, but it showed Lorne and Shoemaker and Downey that he was there all night. I think that helped.

Our trial run was over. Neither Rob nor I had landed a sketch on *SNL*. It was going to be a long summer of stand-up and waiting to see if I still had a job in the fall. I sure hoped so. I wanted that fucking soup at the Omni.

CHAPTER TEN

SNL 1990-1991

After sweating bullets all summer, wondering if I'd get hired back, I finally got the call from *SNL*. Thank God I did, because I hadn't booked any stand-up gigs for the fall, on the hope I'd be heading back to New York. Looking back, that was pretty presumptuous of me considering I hadn't exactly set the world on fire in my trial run the previous season. I would have been doubly fucked if *SNL* hadn't called. Rob also got picked up again, but we were headed back as writer/performers, which still means 95 percent writer, 5 percent performer. Rob was fine with this arrangement. Me, not so much, but this was obviously not a job you turned down.

As a "middle act" on the road (twenty-five to thirty minutes onstage), which meant better than the opener (who gets about a ten-minute set) but not quite headliner (forty-five minutes to an hour) level yet, I had been making $1,000 a week. My work week on the road was Tuesday through Sunday, with Monday as a travel day. So that meant no break, no real day off. It was a rough ride sometimes, and I'd try not to do so many weeks on the road back-to-back. I'd do an off week in the middle of the month so I could do auditions back in L.A. But here's the thing about that *SNL* gig. I thought I'd start out making something crazy, like $10,000 a week. I had about $2,500 a month in bills to pay back then, so I needed to cover at least that, which I was able to do by touring constantly. When I got my option picked up by *SNL,* I was offered the same salary I had been given in my trial run. Not $10,000 a week but a measly (what a great word, right?) $900 a week and a bump to $1,500 if I actually "performed" on the show (fat chance). I was grateful, don't get me wrong. But that $900 came with stress and anxiety from working outside my comfort zone. At least with touring stand-up, I knew what to expect, I knew how to write for myself, I knew how to get laughs. It sucked traveling all the time, but I didn't go to work every day afraid it would be my last.

I went back to the Omni Berkshire Hotel (cue high-pitched singing-angel music) for two weeks of comfort and joy before I was forced to move into a microscopic dogshit apartment. I kept my old apartment in Los Angeles, too, so I could come home on weeks off. This kept my expenses high, but I needed that safety net out in L.A. I had hoped that *SNL* was going to be my ticket to the bank, but this wasn't going to be the case right out of the gate.

When I got to New York, I learned that *SNL* had hired two new feature players: Chris Rock and Chris Farley. I didn't know it at the time, but both ended up becoming great friends of mine. (It's funny, because my best friends have come from high school and *SNL.* Nothing from college, and that's where most people get them; #boringtrivia.) I had heard about each of them through the comedy grapevine and the *SNL* scouts. Rock was a young Eddie Murphy protégé with a dirty, hilarious act. Chris Farley was a sketch player out of Chicago that everyone on staff kept saying had superstar breakout potential (talk about nailing it). Rock lived in Brooklyn so he drove into work every day. I didn't meet him until table read for the first time. Farley was staying at the Omni, so I ran into him in the lobby. I first saw him looking confused there. (I would later realize this was his look 90 percent of the time. Everything confused him . . . ATMs, washing machines, pogo sticks, etc.) I recognized him from his head shot at work and approached him to say hi. I think his response was something along the lines of, "How ya doin'? Chris Farley . . . Gallagher Tent and Awning." Chris always said his name just a hair louder than necessary, with a dip to the side and flip of his hair. (This is a move I saw repeated maybe five thousand times over the course of our friendship. It was his "go-to" move and always got a laugh.) That immediately put my nerves at ease because I could tell right away he wasn't a cocky showbiz asshole. He was scared as hell to be working at *SNL*, just like me. We walked to work together that day, like it was the first day of school. We stopped at an ATM machine so Chris could take out some money. This was something he did all the time. He would usually take out twenty dollars, as he did that afternoon. Noticing this, I said to him, "How long is that twenty bucks going to last you? Make it two hundred so you don't have to hit the ATM again in thirty minutes, man." But that was just how he was. It was his small-town upbringing. Once he pointed at the McDonald's and commented that there was also one back home. This kind of naïveté is why I started calling him Wisconsin Dundee. Everything was new to him, and it was just part of his charm. That was the beginning of our dynamic. Every day I would casually analyze what he did and make fun of it. We did this all day long. And the more he laughed the more I would do it. It fell into place right away and never changed. If I thought for one second it hurt his feelings I would stop, but if I slowed down he would say, "Davey, make fun of me." He knew it wasn't malicious and it was our thing. This is starting to sound like *The Notebook* so I'll move on.

At work he outranked me because he was a full feature player and I was a lowly writer/performer, but he wasn't really aware of that. I had figured out some of the hierarchy in my four-week stint the prior season. It was good that Chris hadn't been hired as a writer/performer like me because he didn't write a lot. But he could be plugged into any sketch and make it better, which made him a very valuable commodity.

That first show of the season was like a typical one the year before—I didn't get jack shit on and I was just always stuck in the writers' room punching up sketches that I wasn't in (sour grapes alert). Luckily, that was becoming more fun since I was starting to get to know peeps, and feeling more comfortable. Our host for the premiere episode was Kyle MacLachlan, star of *Twin Peaks*. The challenge, of course, was coming up with a sketch to do about *Twin Peaks*, which was a massive hit. We just couldn't find the angle. We went in circles for hours and to Rob's credit he finally cracked the code in the eleventh hour. I think the idea was for Kyle to have solved a murder, but to continue to look for the culprit because he doesn't want the show to end. Jim Downey was very happy when Rob came up with that idea. This in turn made me super jealous. Rob was getting the full "for he's a jolly good fellow" treatment while I was getting the "why did we hire you back" stink-eye. I do remember that in that *Twin Peaks* sketch, Chris Farley played a prisoner in handcuffs. He barely had anything to do but he was still extremely watchable. He made his part funnier than it should have been, even when he wasn't given anything funny to do. I could see right away what everyone had been talking about. This guy had star potential, for sure. He was immediately interesting to watch. Meanwhile I'm off to the side gathering dust.

For the third show that season, George Steinbrenner was the host. I am from Arizona so I didn't understand or give a shit why this guy was hosting. Everyone around me seemed to understand perfectly well, because they were all Yankees fans. All I cared about was how I was going to plug a sixty-five-year-old guy who can't act into my "hilarious" sketch ideas. I'm pretty sure I wound up writing a Weekend Update bit for myself again. Dennis Miller was still hosting Weekend Update, and he was a fan of my writing and would always encourage me to write something for that bit. That was nice, in a place where no one gave a fuck. It wasn't like anyone was outright mean, it was just that the other writers and performers had their own shit to worry about and they didn't want to get fired, either. So when you didn't get a sketch on, folks weren't sad for you. They were quietly doing mental cartwheels because of the schadenfreude festival around the seventeenth floor. Not super great for the old ego. I was quickly starting to understand where Lovitz had been coming from that first time we met. It was amazing how fast I turned into that same guy.

My Weekend Update that week was about the looming war in the Persian Gulf, since Saddam Hussein had invaded Kuwait in August 1990. It involved two dolls, and I used them to explain the war in simple terms. One doll was my brother Bryan, and he represented Iraq. He was a big bully. The other doll was me, and represented Kuwait. I acted out Bryan/Iraq punching me, holding me/Kuwait down, spitting and sucking it back up. The United States was my mom coming in to break it up. It was a pretty funny bit but nothing special; still, at least I had gotten something on. I was on the show. Now people in Arizona might believe me when I said I was on *Saturday Night Live*.

The next show was very memorable for two reasons. The first

is that the show instigated a sketch idea that I later ran with, and the second reason is that it included one of my favorite, and one of the most memorable, *SNL* sketches of all time—the Chippendales. Patrick Swayze was the host that week. He was a supercool dude, and nice to everyone. He was another guy, like Baldwin, who was up for anything. On Tuesday night when we wrote sketches, the host came in between 5 and 6 P.M., said hello, heard a few pitches, and then went to dinner at Orso. Usually, Lorne would choose a few cast members to go along for the meal to fill the table, and to make sure the host had a good time. I got asked to attend this dinner often, and I usually went. It was that tough position to be in—I wanted to be around Lorne and the host and possibly be amusing at dinner, but by going it meant that I was pushing back my writing session even later. I never drank at those dinners because I knew I had to write afterward. (I can't picture not drinking at them now.)

On this particular night at around nine thirty or ten, Patrick came back with us and did a little face time with each writer, heard their ideas, and gave his feedback off the top of his head. This kind of quick meeting can be very valuable, because this is when you find out whether or not your host can do a German accent, if he'd be up to play a hillbilly, or any other bit of useful information that will help your sketch . . . or sometimes kill it on the spot. I've seen sketches be 90 percent done only to get killed when the host casually says, "Oh, I don't want to do anything political." Then your sketch is dead on arrival. It's heartbreaking. On this night, I asked where Patrick Swayze was because I had been out of my office when he came by. I heard he was in the writers' room, so I headed over. I peeked in and was surprised to see Patrick sitting alone and just reading, without being smothered by writers or cast members star-fucking him. Now I had *my* chance to star-fuck him! Plus, I had some wispy ideas that I wanted to run past him. So I started to walk in and out of nowhere this publicist stepped in front of me and blocked the doorway so I couldn't get in. I looked at her arm, in front of my face, and then turned to her with sort of a quizzical "What the fuck is going on?" look. She said, "Hi, can I help you?" And I said, "Oh, hi, just wanted to chat with Patrick for a second." And then she said those three magical words that I'll never forget: "Annnnddd youuuu arrrre?" I was a little taken aback. I had never run into any resistance walking up to a host, especially in the writers' room. "Oh, sorry, I'm David Spade." "Right, and this is regardingggggggggggggggg . . . ?" I go, "I'm a writer, and I wanted to talk to Patrick about a sketch." In my head I was wondering why I was talking to this stranger who didn't care to tell me who the hell *she* was. As you might have guessed, her response was "Yeah . . . um . . . he's . . . swamped right now. Can you come back later? It's just nuts right now." I peered over her arm. "Isn't that him sitting there reading *People* magazine?" And of course she fired back, "Yeah, it's a really bad time." I just gave up. I walked away confused but laughing at how ridiculous that attitude was. That convo stuck in my head for a full year until I tweaked it and it became one of my best-known sketches . . . "The Receptionist."

Jim Downey wrote the famous Chippendales sketch that made Chris into a breakout star. It was only the fourth show of the season, but after that, there was no turning back. It was that kind of dream part that everybody wishes they could get—it used all of Chris's strengths, including his physical comedy, his surprising dancing ability, and his sweet and vulnerable acting. The real unsung hero of this sketch was Patrick Swayze. He played his role so perfectly, and it made Farley even funnier. Swayze had an impressive dancing background, and he was this perfect male specimen with the ripped abs and long hair. And then there was Chris the polar opposite, a sloppy, out-of-work, chubby everyman. To put both of them side by side, auditioning for a spot as a Chippendales dancer, was just comedy gold. But this was one of those sketches that had almost no margin of error. It was funny from the concept to read-through to dress rehearsal to air, and it never faltered.

A lot of sketches are hilarious in read-through and when you put them on their feet and act them out, they lose something and it doesn't quite work. Sometimes no one can put their finger on why; it was just "better at read-through." Some sketches barely squeak through at read-through and gain momentum during the week with better jokes and then great performances blow it through the roof on Saturday night. This one everyone had high hopes for from the start, and it came through big-time. I still quote this sketch when Kevin Nealon announces his decision and addresses both of them saying, "Adrian . . . Barney . . ." Adrian was a perfect name for Patrick's character and Barney was spot-on for Chris. In fact, he should have been named that in real life. I also loved the moment after Farley realizes he isn't getting the job and starts making sexy faces at Nealon to try to change his mind. Kevin says, "Barney, Barney . . . it's over, Barney." It still makes me crack up. I think many people of our generation would say it's one of their favorite *Saturday Night Live* sketches ever. It was an instant classic.

So now Chris was off and running, and every writer started putting him in every sketch because he would score for sure. The pressure on him was instant.

Around this time, maybe late fall, one of my other buddies got hired: Adam Sandler. Adam was a comic from New Hampshire who also lived near me in the Valley. We had met at a comedy club a few years earlier and hung out here and there. Adam was and is such an easy guy to chill with. We would get together and drink, do sets at the clubs, or play tennis. Rob was usually around, and so was Judd Apatow, who lived with Sandler at this time. Judd was another cool dude with a funny act. Allen Covert also lived there, as well as Jack Giarraputo, who has been Sandler's producing partner for years in Happy Madison films. But at that point, we were just a bunch of young and struggling idiots in the Valley trying to get drunk, get laid, and get some stage time. Dennis Miller, Rob, Fred Wolf, and I had all tried to push Sandler on Lorne and the talent scouts whenever we could . . . not that we had such great job security ourselves, but he was a pal. Well, he came in and was a workhorse, a great addition to the show right away. He knew Chris Rock some, so he shared an office with him. I shared an office with Farley. Mind you, these offices were like ten by ten feet. Not only were they tiny, but you also had to walk through our office to get to theirs, which was frustrating 1 percent of the time, but superfun the other 99 percent.

Adam was always very good about doing his homework. He would get to his office and work on an Update piece or a sketch all night long. Robert Smigel, who was one of the best writers we had, would write with him a lot. I was a bit envious (of course) because I never had anyone strong on my team. Adam was such a good writer himself that the combination of him and Smigel was lethal. They would be in there laughing like crazy and I would be at my desk staring at my yellow legal pad (no laptops back then, kiddos) trying to conjure up some shitty bit and usually failing. Adam was perfect for the show because he had an arsenal of characters. When we were bored, he would crank-call people and act like he was a woman, or do a Bernie Brillstein accent or whatever. We would all just laugh our asses off. He was very quick on the phone, which is actually a good indication of whether someone is really funny. I always picture myself back then just sitting at my boring, wooden, basic desk with my yellow legal pad, with nothing on the pages, trying to come up with something. I didn't have a ton of characters or really even a ton of ideas. I thought I did when I started but as the shows peel away it's like déjà vu on Monday when they give you another host and you have to think of another fucking sketch for him that no one's done in the last twenty-five years. It starts to

get hard. I think Conan O'Brien explained to me once my weekend update bits needed a "concept" and explained it can't be just
jokes. I swear this was news to me and changed the way I wrote.
I just wasn't aware. One disadvantage I had was I wasn't worldly
enough. Or even stately (not even a real term). I was so naïve about
East Coast shit. The accents in New York are different than New
Hampshire, etc. Also, I didn't come from a religious background
so knew nothing of Jewish or Irish Catholic cultures. It was all
foreign to me so I couldn't mine it for jokes like they did. That
frustrated me.

Farlz didn't write much, or read for that matter, so he was
usually very bored sitting at his desk. He would get antsy like
a kindergartner. I remember him saying, "David, turn around."
I wouldn't answer, so he'd start again. "David, turn around, it's
funny." I'd say, "I promise it's not going to be worth it." And he
would say, "No, I've got a bit I'm going to try out on you; it's a
good one." I'd answer, "If this is Fat Guy in a Little Coat again,
I'm not into it. I think that peaked on the charts about a year ago."
And he'd go, "No, it's not. It's a whole new thing I'm doing!" So
I'd slowly stop writing, put my pen down, turn around in my chair,
and he'd have my little Levi jacket on and say, "Fat Guy in a Little
Coat . . . DAVID, DON'T YOU GIVE UP ON IT!" And we'd
laugh cuz he would really sell it the ninety-eighth time he did it.
Then I'd say, "Let's take a break. You want to go eat?" The answer
was always yes, and so we'd grab Rock and Sandler and head down
to Wally's & Joseph's . . . the mobsterish Italian and steak place
within a mile of 30 Rock. Which I mentioned before. Some of my
best memories of this gig are from walking down to that restaurant
there. Tim Meadows came with us once in a while, and sometimes
Schneider. It was always just a band of dipshits walking down the
street laughing, blowing off steam, and de-stressing in the middle
of New York City.

Chris would always try to make us laugh, usually by stopping girls and asking them if they had any ID, or by doing push-ups on the street and telling them he was a personal trainer. I remember once we saw a pretty girl walking in front of us and Adam said to Farley, "Chris, you should talk to her." Right then, she hailed a cab. Chris ran up behind her and climbed in the cab with her, saying something like, "Hey, heading uptown?" and started to laugh. The girl immediately started kicking and screaming at Farley. "Get the fuck out of here!" It was pretty funny because if you didn't know he was famous, he was just an obnoxious dude possibly trying to attack you.

Tom Hanks hosted on the eighth show of that season. This was super-exciting for all of us. Hanks is a massive star and stays at that level no matter what he does. I naturally was out of ideas, and some mere whisper of an idea was definitely not good enough for a star of his caliber. So I decided to just go with the flow of the Monday meeting, bullshitting my way through it.

A lot of people, including myself, gave fake ideas when we couldn't think of anything fast enough after the last show. Rob would come in and say something like "You're a caveman afraid of caves, or a pilot afraid of flying . . ." those types of lame pitches that always made me laugh because they actually sort of sound like real ideas, even though we all knew they weren't. And every Monday they would get used and never written. Farley usually went at the end of the Monday meeting and would fuss and struggle and act all OCD nuts waiting to say his idea. Which was always shitty. Which was half the fun. Watching him twist and turn in the wind while it would get closer and closer to his turn, watching him grabbing at the carpet and holding his sweaty, crumpled legal pad.

Finally, his turn in the Hanks meeting came. Lorne pointed at him, "Chris. Anything for Tom?"

Chris snapped his head up and pulled his hair . . . and finally spat out, "Um, hey Tom Hanks." (Saying his full name, like a total psycho.) "Um uh, I was thinking, you know that movie *Marty*, with Ernest Borgnine? Um, maybe doing something on that . . ."

Silence. Everyone stared. Then Lorne shredded him with, "Well, this is the week. Everyone will be looking for our *Marty* sketch." Cue to the whole room laughing because *Marty* is a movie from 1954 that no one gives a fuck about and the pitch makes absolutely no sense, which is what made it all so hilar.

When we left the meeting to go eat, I got into Chris's head immediately.

"Chris, seriously, what the fuck? *Marty*? Are you retarded?"

"Shut up, David. It was my bluff."

"Bluff? Why didn't you say a cowboy afraid of cows. Or literally any idea from the last thirty years?"

"Fuck off. All your ideas were shitty too."

"Tom Hanks was so mad."

It was priceless.

Luckily though, that meeting wasn't a total disaster for me. It turned out, Tommy Hanks had a few ideas of his own. This happens sometimes. Maybe the host has met with some writer friends before they came to New York, or if they were on a sitcom, perhaps those writers have given them ideas. Sometimes certain hosts are just comedically inclined, and they offer up some sketch ideas or impressions they can do. These little nuggets are very valuable to a writer, but since most of the writers were caught up in their own great sketches, ideas from hosts fell on deaf ears. Well . . . not for Spade. I had no ideas so my ears were *wiiiiide* open. I knew that writing a sketch with the host always tipped the scales in your favor. The idea that Hanks tossed out that I jumped on was called Subway Surfing. Everyone else sort of checked out during his pitch, but I sat there soaking it all in. The concept was that Hanks and all the cast would ride the subway around the boroughs of New York "surfing" along inside and singing a song about it. Once he told me that there was a song involved, I knew I was in over my head. I could barely manage to write a sketch from beginning to middle to end . . . and I had absolutely no business trying to write a song. But Hanks was happy that one of the writers liked his idea, so he had a lot of enthusiasm. I didn't have the heart to tell him that the only reason I went for it was that it had surfing in the title—still clinging to my Arizona, OP-shorts-wearing, skateboard-riding roots.

The next step was actually putting pen to yellow legal pad and writing it. I'd sit with Tom for a little bit and we'd hash it out and then he'd be pulled in fifty different directions and I'd be left to hammer out the details and try to make it all make sense. I needed to finish a rough draft and let him scope it out, take any ideas he threw out and implement them, then hand it in by deadline. This should have been simple enough, except Hanks wasn't aware that I couldn't really write. I wasn't Smigel or Jack Handy or Conan O'Brien and I didn't really know what I was doing. Well, I somehow finished it by read-through and put it on the pile. The best part: seeing the writers listed as HANKS/SPADE in the top corner. That made me feel legit, for the first time since I got there. If I had a camera phone back then I certainly would have snapped a sneaky pic and posted it on Instabrag but I didn't even have a cell phone at that point. (Yes, I'm that old.) A bit later the read-through started and "Subway Surfing" was on the docket. I was sweating even more than usual, because I really wanted this one to do well, for me but also for Hanks. (Well, really for me. He's fine.) We read it together and sang the song. Tom gave it everything. He gave everything 100 percent all the time, but this sketch he gave 101 percent. It was probably a 7 out of 10 on the laugh meter, more conceptual and fun than hilarious, if I am being honest. It was by no means a home run for the final cut and I knew it. So off I went to Wally's & Joseph's, all by myself, sweating it out, pondering why I was losing my hair. I sprinted back to see if the sketch was on the board and it was! Victory! Then came the hard part: all the department heads asked me to help put the sketch together—wigs, makeup, set. I bluffed my way through it and ran to Tom for the tricky questions. We threw it up at dress rehearsal and sang our hearts out but we just didn't quite nail it. I could tell in the middle we were dead in the water. The crowd liked it, but there just weren't enough laughs. Much to no one's surprise, our sketch didn't make it to air. I was bummed, but he was a class act the whole way. He grabbed me later at the after party and said, "Hey, we tried . . . I thought it was funny." We laughed and I felt a little better, for about five minutes, when I had to start thinking of material for the next host.

One of the impressions in my arsenal (arsenal meaning two impressions) was of Michael J. Fox. When I learned he was the next host, I was stoked. I knew this could be a big week for me with this in my back pocket. I really needed a solid showing. I still hadn't really done jack shit that season and my buddy Rob had already scored big with Copy Machine guy (with Sting, of all people), and I was in a jealous frenzy. Things were already getting a bit prickly between Rob and me and this didn't help. I thought him writing himself as the lead in a sketch wasn't cool at all, because we had been told to write for other people. The fact that the sketch had already been on twice (another ballsy move! writing two sketches with yourself in the lead!) by the time he ran it with Sting felt totally unfair. I was quickly reminded that nothing was fair about *SNL*. Of course, if the sketch had been mine, I probably would have been more than happy to bend the rules. But generally, I'm a rule follower. I respect the system. Unfortch it takes ballsy shit like that to get ahead in showbiz (and life) and I'm just not built like that. *SNL* was the wrong place to be Mr. Polite, Dudley Do-Right. (This is an old reference lost on you youngsters who probably won't like this book anyway.) Rob, Sandler, and Farley were blowing past me on rocket ships and I was dead scared of getting shitcanned. I hoped Mr. Michael J. Fox would lift me out of my tailspin.

At the Monday meeting, I met Michael for the first time. He was very cool, excited, and up for anything—like I said, the best kind of host. He knew someone on staff did an impression of him and that it would probably be in the show and he seemed fine with that idea, so my spirits were starting to lift. Smigel came up with a sketch about child stars gone bad planning a bank robbery and there was a rumor going around that I'd play Fox. Now I was stoked. I was going to get a few crumbs this week and they would keep me from blowing my brains out and more important, would save my job. (I guess the job was less important than dying?) That child actor sketch was written and hilarious at read-through. Michael played Danny Bonaduce, Chris Farley played Mindy Cohn from *Facts of Life (JUST DO IT RIPPY)*, and I played Michael J. Fox. I then got a call to go into Lorne's office to talk about the monologue, which I was also rumored to be in. Maybe my days of "Please, sir, may I have some more," Oliver Twist–like starving for screen time were coming to an end? When I got to Lorne's office, he told me that I was indeed going to appear in the monologue, along with Michael and Dana Carvey, all playing . . . Michael J. Fox in a cool *Back to the Future* bit. At this point, I was over the moon. But then Lorne dropped the whammy. He explained that because I was new and the audience wasn't familiar with me, Dana Carvey had to come out first. And, to add insult to injury, I had to coach him on how to do the Michael J. Fox impression. Basically, I had to give Carvey the best thing I knew how to do, and then follow him on and look like a copycat. Shit. I fell in line like a good soldier and went to Dana's office to walk him through, and he locked it immediately, as predicted. Dana was ten times better at impressions than anyone at *SNL*, so that was not a shocker. I went to bed a bit grumbly that night.

At dress rehearsal the next night, the monologue was fine, but the sketch about child stars was crazy, because when I was playing opposite Fox, dressed as Fox, Michael started laughing. That always makes a sketch crush. When we did it on air, it worked, but Fox didn't laugh this time, and a little spark was lost. It was still a big moment for me, but I couldn't help wish that the dress version was what had made it to air.

As if things couldn't get better than being on air twice in one week (Yay! $1,500 paycheck that week!!), I finally had my very first sketch make it to air. It was called "Not Gettin' Any." It was a talk show consisting of a bunch of guys sitting around complaining about not getting laid. Very original, right? I was on my own, totally in charge of wardrobe, wigs, set design, line readings, and getting all my cuts and changes to the script to the cue card department in time for the live show. This was quite an undertaking, and I quickly realized you have to pace yourself and pick your fights in these situations. You have to stay focused on the decisions that really matter—and those are the ones about the jokes. When someone grabs you in the hall and says, "What kind of couch should you guys be sitting on . . . is it modern or more of a cozy L-shaped one at home?" just say the first thing that pops into your head or outsource that shit to someone who is better than you at those kinds of details. I sucked at those decisions.

It played okay. It didn't set the world on fire. But of course, the thing I remember most fondly is something my boy Farley did. I had Chris Farley in the sketch because he was a score machine and I needed him. I wrote a line that had him asking a girl if he could "lay her down in the tall grass and let me do my stuff." That's a line from a Fleetwood Mac song but I knew he'd say it in a funny way and make it work. During rehearsals he pulled me aside and said, "Davey, in that sketch you wrote, what if I said, 'I have a weight problem, hell my folks don't even know. I swallow a lot of aggression, along with a lot of pizzas' . . . Can I say that?" And I said, "Shit yeah, that's pretty funny." So I added those new lines in. The sketch made it through dress rehearsal and by some miracle got on the live show. I was stoked it was finally happening. As I was walking onto the set Saturday night, Farley grabbed me and said, "This is going to be great, Davey." And I said, "Yeah, I hope so. And that stuff you added killed." And then he got a weird look on his face as we are walking along before grabbing my arm really hard and whispering, "Psss psss sss . . . *Stripes*." With the band playing and all the noise in the studio, I sort of yelled, "What's that?" And he sheepishly said, "Ummm, I think that was from *Stripes*."

I got a chill down my spine and it all hit me. "Wait a minute, CHRIS . . . those lines you gave me are something John Candy said in the movie *Stripes*???" I was like, WAIT . . . WHAAAT? He started hemming and hawing: "Aww Davey, it's okay, no one will know." The look on his face was one of panic and guilt. I knew you couldn't use a line from a movie in a sketch. That was stealing. My stomach dropped. And then Joe Dicso, the stage manager, yelled, "David, sit down! We got ten seconds . . . five . . . four . . . three . . ." I glared at Chris and he walked to his seat knowing he had done something wrong. The sketch went off fine and afterward he grabbed me really hard because he knew he was in trouble with me. "David, don't be mad at me, it's fine." "Chris, people are going to think I stole it because I wrote it." And then he started laughing because he knew it was wrong but didn't really care. He started singing, "Won't you lay me down in the tall grass and let me do my stuff . . ." out of nervous energy. I couldn't help but laugh at this moron. Stuff like that always, always got him out of trouble, with me and everyone else. Scenarios like that are sort of what turned into the movie *Tommy Boy,* or at least parts of it . . . which we will get to in a bit.

Overall the Michael J. Fox episode was a victory, but I still didn't think I had made enough of an impact on the show and the season was almost over. I wasn't totally worth keeping yet. It could still go either way, and could easily be back to doing stand-up at the Arkansas Rib Tickler by June.

CHAPTER ELEVEN
SNL 1991-1992

The summer after my first full season, I was back driving around Los Angeles in my used Acura Legend waiting to find out if I was going back. I had gotten rid of my dinky New York apartment on the corner of Eighty-Fifth Street and West End Avenue, because I couldn't get anyone on the show to tell me if I was going to be hired back three months later. In hindsight, this seems very stupid. It was such a hassle to move all of my shit out of my apartment, get it back to L.A., then find a place back in New York that I could rent month-to-month, wait for the cable guy, find a new bed, rehang the autographed picture of myself, blah blah blah. It was never worth it. If I thought for one second I'd be somewhat famous or have money one day, I would never have lifted a finger and just rolled the dice and hoped for the best. Those just add to the intangible (but somewhat tangible) things that make *Saturday Night Live* a stressful place that drives people crazy.

I finally got the call to come back, which was a huge sigh of relief personally and professionally. I was very driven at that time and wanted to do well in my field that everyone told me not to pursue. I had such a massive chip on my shoulder about being an underdog from Arizona with no show business connections. I had to see how far I could get. Add to that the fact that I hated disappointing the people who were trying to hang in there with me back home. I'd get a lot of calls from friends and other comedian buddies saying, "Dude, I waited up." Which meant, they stayed up all the way to the end of the show hoping to catch me once . . . and got nothing. Sometime I'd go onstage at the end when the host and the band wave good-bye, just so people would see that I hadn't been fired. I used to joke with Farley that some weeks, I counted that as a sketch.

We launched our first show that season with none other than the G.O.A.T., Michael Jordan. He was an upbeat, fun guy . . . but also very intimidating. It was business as usual the first show back, with me appearing in one sketch with one line. Actually it wasn't even a line, it was a reaction shot, which I counted as a line. The sketch took place in the 1960s and we were a shitty all-white basketball team that was very resistant to adding Michael Jordan to our roster because he was black. No one would pass the ball to Jordan, even though he was clearly the best guy on the team. It was very funny. At halftime, Michael gave an impassioned speech about teamwork, until Mike Myers told him, "We don't want you on the team." Taken aback Jordan said, "You all really don't want me on the team?" And then he looked at me and asked, "Even you, Pee Wee?" I quickly averted my eyes in shame. I got a laugh, that tiny rush of adrenaline. I wanted to run to Lorne and say, "Look,

Mr. Hitler will see you now. *Photograph courtesy of the author.*

Opening for Ray Charles in New York. My first trip to NYC and my highest paid gig, $1,500. *Photograph courtesy of the author.*

With my buddy Dennis Miller and his mullet. *Photograph courtesy of Tribune Media Company.*

And you are . . . ? The late great Phil Hartman doing Sinatra.
Photograph courtesy of Ng for Edie Baskin.

Me trying to avoid permanent residence in a van. *Photograph courtesy of Ng for Edie Baskin.*

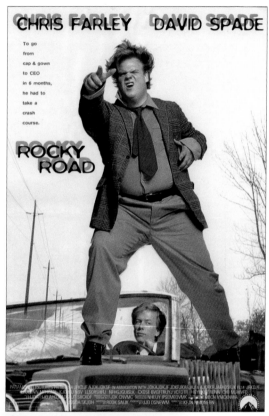

The first poster and title of what would become *Tommy Boy*. *Photograph courtesy of Paramount Pictures.*

Black Sheep in between cop car takes. Frying in 103-degree heat. Umbrellas like Puff Daddy. *Photograph courtesy of Paramount Pictures.*

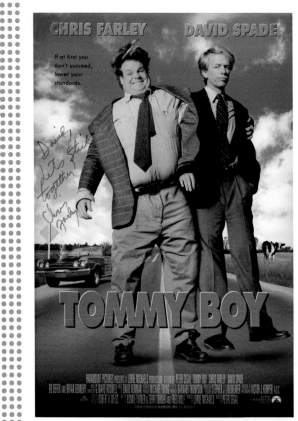

Tommy Boy poster. The movie that changed everything. Notice Chris signed it. I signed one for him too. *Photograph courtesy of Paramount Pictures.*

Tense in a limo after *SNL* on the way to the airport for a rough *Tommy Boy* Sunday shoot. *Photograph courtesy of the author.*

Hollywood Minute with Kevin Nealon and Steve Martin. Steve was very cool to participate in this. Love this guy. *Photograph courtesy of Ng for Edie Baskin.*

```
SHOW #1392                              HOST: DAVID SPADE
AIR DATE: MARCH 12, 2005                MUSICAL GUEST: JACK JOHNSON

PRELIMINARY RUNDOWN:
CNN COLD OPEN (W/VT)          punch up
OPENING MONTAGE (VT)           Martha
CAPITAL ONE MONOLOGUE
WOOMBA (VT)
CELEBRITY ROAST   Owen - dick nose
   BAND SHOT/BUMPER (W/VT)
   Commercial #1 [Net/Tease/Local]

DESIGN COUPLE
   BAND SHOT/NEXT WEEK PROMO (W/VT)
   Commercial #2 [Net/Tease/Local]

STUNTMEN   Horatio Vin
DEAF JUDGE (VT)
DIRTBALL & BURNOUT CONVENTION   more jokes
   BAND SHOT/BUMPER (W/VT)       meth lab free class
   Commercial #3 [Net/Tease/Local]   for kiddies

DAVID INTRO &
JACK JOHNSON "Sitting, Waiting, Wishing"
   BUMPER/MUSIC BILLBOARD (W/VT)
   Commercial #4/
   N.I./Station Break

UPDATE (W/VT)           Interpreter
   Commercial #5 [Net/Tease/Local]

JINGLE SINGERS   out fit ad lib
   BAND SHOT/BUMPER (W/VT)
   Commercial #6 [Net/Tease/Local]

RECORD COMPANY ——— new rap
MYSTERIOUS PHENOMENA (VT)
UPSKIRT REPORT (W/VT) ———
   BAND SHOT/BUMPER (W/VT)
   Commercial #7 [Net/Tease/Local]
SPIDERMAN
BEAR CITY: GARAGE BAND (VT)
UPS GUY (W/VT) ———            A
   BAND SHOT/BUMPER (W/VT)
   N.I./Station Break

DAVID INTRO &
JACK JOHNSON "Mudfootball"
   Commercial #8 [Local Avail]

FIRST TIME IN THE JOINT ——— more jokes
   Commercial #9 [Local Avail]

GOODNIGHTS & CREDITS (W/VT)
```

SNL rundown sheet from hosting. *Photograph courtesy of the author.*

Skippy. *Photograph courtesy of the author.*

Bryan, Andy, and me. *Photograph courtesy of the author.*

Bryan, Andy, my mom, and me at the old Malibu house. *Photograph courtesy of the author.*

Bryan, me, Mom, and Andy. And Princess. Must be the '70s. *Photograph courtesy of the author.*

Lorne, I got a laugh without even saying anything. I'm magical!"
But I opted against it. Instead I just wrote it in my diary.

The one thing that stands out most about Michael Jordan hosting *SNL* is how many people wanted his autograph. I'd never seen a
line like the one outside his dressing room. It was the cast, the writers, the crew, everyone. We were supposedly cynical and cool, but I
remember seeing Al Franken standing there holding three basket-
balls to sign. Finally, Lorne put a stop to it. It was the only time a
sign had to be posted at 30 Rock that said "NO MORE AUTO-
GRAPHS." How embarrassing. I was waiting to get a picture at
the end of the week. My strategy went out the fucking window.

Our next host was Jeff Daniels. Jeff is one of those everyman
types that is sometimes hard to write for because he is such a talented actor that he blends in a bit. It can be hard to find the angle
to hang a sketch on (I'll take any excuse I can get). He's not super-
handsome. He's not the fat guy. He's not angry or pushy. So . . . he
seemed destined for sketches that had him cast as the husband in a
family bit or the host of a game show. But we tried. Unfortunately,
what could have been a pretty straightforward week turned into
something pretty traumatic in the office of 30 Rock.

On the Friday night before the show, Jeff was scheduled to get
a face mask made. For those of us who have had this done, it can be
a terrifying experience. If the makeup department wants to make a
dummy that looks like you, or there needs to be a shot of your head
blowing up, a plasterlike substance is poured on your face to create a mold that can then be used to sculpt a replica. This process is
nerve-racking and plays on all of our primal fears. I've had it done,
and I totally freaked out.

First, a stocking cap is placed over your hair to make it smooth.
Then this white crap that looks like Bisquick gets spread all over
your face. Two straws get stuck up your nose so you can breathe,
because your mouth gets covered with this junk, too. I had been

warned that the worst part was when your ears were covered. I said, "Hey, guys I'm not a pussy." (I am.) "I get what's going on." When the time came I said, "Just go slowly . . . I'm not freaking out." I realized what was happening, and I started taking deep breaths to get ready. I was okay when they covered my eyes, but then again, as if the makeup artists were talking to a child, they'd say, "We're just covering your ears, don't freak out." I said, "Guys, I get it, I get it. I don't care. Just do it." About five seconds into it, I got a rush of anxiety and started screaming. I demanded some Valium, which of course someone had because clearly this was a common occurrence (and everyone involved in showbiz is a drug addict). They stuffed it down my gullet before they closed it up with plaster. It took everything I had to calm myself down enough to let them finish and then wait the fifteen minutes it takes for the plaster to harden. It is hard to explain why the freak-out happens so often, but I think it is because your body goes into panic mode thinking you are being buried alive. That's all I can figure. Well, poor me.

Anyway, for some sketch we needed a Jeff Daniels doll. He was told to show up at 7 P.M. in the makeup room for the face mask process. As the story goes, the makeup artists put the straws up Jeff's nose and slowly applied the pancake batter as per usual. He was very cool about it all, even when they covered the eyes, ears, and mouth . . . knowing he didn't have a big choice in the matter. I guess he wasn't a total pussy like me. After waiting fifteen minutes for it to harden, the makeup artists started to try to peel it off. Usually the mask comes off in one sticky piece. It feels pretty gross, like your skin is being removed. Well, not this time. After a few minutes of struggling, it became clear there was a MAJOR problem. This wasn't makeup on Jeff's face. It was some kind of actual plaster.

Everyone immediately went into panic mode. This shit was not coming off his face. Everyone started yelling at him so he could

hear beneath the plaster, "Don't worry, Jeff! Just a few more minutes, Jeff!" even though they knew this was not true at all. Some
folks snuck off to call Lorne at dinner and ask something to the
effect of "WHAT THE FUCK DO WE DO, BOSS?!" Lorne
called a plastic surgeon to come to 30 Rock to suss out the situation. By the way, it had been about a half hour at this point, and
Jeff Daniels now realized that something had gone terribly wrong.
He wrote on a piece of paper, "I'm feeling sick." In return, he got
this little nugget: "Don't throw up or you'll die! The puke has nowhere to go!" Thanks, that's COMFORTING!!

Two hours later, the plastic surgeon comes in. They peel the
plaster off Jeff's forehead as far as it will go, but his eyebrows and
eyelashes are stuck in it. Doing the grimmest move possible, but
the only option, the surgeon sticks an X-Acto knife down the front
of the mask and carefully cuts off Jeff's eyebrows and eyelashes so
the doctor can get the plaster off the rest of his face. I can't imagine
the relief and the pain Jeff must have felt at that point. Everyone
was worried that the show might get canceled the next day. Daniels
was traumatized. They fixed him up medically and sent him home.
To his credit, and the reason I love Jeff Daniels to this day, is that
he showed up the next day and did the whole show without being a
drama queen (which is called for when there's actual drama), and he
didn't sue or bitch or talk about it incessantly like I'm sure I would
have. He just showed up, busted his ass through every sketch like
nothing happened, and did a great job. If you watch that old show,
you can see his eyebrows were painted on. To this day, it is still a
mystery how that mix-up happened in the makeup department. I
have my theories (they involve aliens and 9/11).

That season, I had another chance to trot out one of my
impressions—my old standby from the suitcase days. Tom Petty.
I was pretty excited to meet the dude in person. I even thought he
might be excited to meet me, since I had been doing him for years.

I forgot that sometimes impressions aren't 100 percent flattering, so the person being imitated might not be head over heels in love when they see it. Being the genius sketch writer I am, I couldn't think of a sketch that would include an impression of him. Here I had a chance to do one of the three killer impressions in my arsenal, and I was blowing it. I say three because that's a pretty low number. I should have had at least ten, but I was a little light in that department. Luckily I made up for it with snarkiness! (Said like a used car salesman.) So, on Wednesday night after read-through, in a shocking turn of events, I realized I had nothing in the show. I spent the next two days wandering around the halls watching everyone else work on their sketches like little elves, while I took my place as the resident loser. During the dress rehearsal, I had a bit of a brainstorm while sipping on an Amstel Light. I ran into Tom Petty's dressing room with my beer balls and said, "Can I talk to Tom?" Unlike Patrick Swayze, his people let me right in. I said, "Tom, here's my pitch . . . I have been a fan of yours forever and I actually do an impression of you. I've done it on the show. Is there any way when they go to commercial on the live show, you and I can sing together? They always cut to that boring G. E. Smith playing guitar for thirty seconds or however long they need to kill time before a commercial. I think that should be us." He stared at me for a second and then leaned over to pick up his guitar and said, "Sure, what song?" I was like, *Holy fuck. He's going along with it!* I said, "Well, I can't really sing. I just make noises." And he goes, "What about 'Breakdown'?" And I said, "I love it but it's got too long of an intro. We only have about thirty seconds. How about 'I Need to Know'?" And he said, "Let me see how it goes again." And he starts strumming his guitar, which of course put me in fan-girl mode because it was so cool. He says, "There's sixteen bars and then you come in." I said, "Well, I don't know how that works because I don't know music, so, can I just start at the words and then you jump in?" And there was a pause and he goes, "Sure, we'll figure it out. I'll just follow you." And then to make things even cooler, Ben, his keyboard player, said, "Can I play, too?"

Meanwhile, in my drunken haze I have not run this by ONE PERSON from Lorne's office. This is fully unauthorized, but put an Amstel Light and a half in me and look the fuck out! I'm on a mission! My only snag, aside from breaking all the rules, was one mercy line that was thrown to me in a sketch after read-through. I guess someone felt sorry for me. Depending on where the sketch fell, my master Tom Petty plan should have gone off no problem. And, in pure Spade fashion, it turned out to be a problem.

The "band shot," as they call it, is usually scheduled before a commercial. The camera pans from the actors at the end of a sketch over to the band jamming until commercial break. These are strategically placed throughout the show. On this particular evening there was only one and it happened to be right after the sketch I was in. When I drunkenly bombarded Tom Petty with this idea, I had forgotten I had one line in the show. Now I realized when timing it out, I had probably sixty seconds to do my line, run around the corner, throw on my Tom Petty hat, glasses, sideburns, and fringed leather jacket and get settled before the live band shot started. I had to run around during the live show and tell the actual band what was going on, then tell Tom Petty where to stand, basically tell everyone what was happening BUT LORNE. Tom and I decided that I would start right at the beginning of "I Need to Know" right when the red light went on on the camera, meaning we were live. I informed the cameraman that instead of panning over to me, to just cut to me when the sketch was over.

So I did my sketch and nailed my line (debatable) and sprinted over by the band as soon as I was off camera. I quickly threw on my gear with my heart pounding because I am terrified to sing . . . and more terrified that Lorne is going to rip me a new one. Tom Petty walked out, holding his guitar. He looked over at me with a cocked eyebrow that said, "You ready?" I realized we probably should have run this in rehearsal because I had no idea what to do next. Before I knew it, the camera turned to me and the red light went on. I instantly screamed, "WELL THE TALK ON THE STREET SAYS YOU MIGHT GO SOLO . . ." in my best Tom Petty voice. Then I heard Petty kick in with the guitar that I'm so famil- iar with and I jumped on the second line, "A GOOD FRIEND OF MINE SAW YOU LEAVING THROUGH THE BACK DOOR . . ." More guitar, adrenaline going, crazy . . . Now the chorus, "I NEED TO KNOW . . ." And bless Tom Petty's heart he threw in a background vocal, "I NEED TO KNOW . . ." And we went back and forth for another ten seconds until the red light went off and we were clearly at a commercial. I stepped back from the mic and Tom quickly pointed to me and said, "Keep going!" I leaned forward and we belted out the rest of the song for the audi- ence. We did the whole thing; I was horrible but had such a blast. I felt like I was really in the band for a minute. I see why guys like to be in bands. It was ridiculously fun. At the end of the show, I even scurried up for the "good night" curtain call because I felt like I added something to the show that night. Surprisingly, Lorne never said a word about it.

A few shows after that, Macaulay Culkin was the host. This is when I finally developed my encounter with Patrick Swayze's publi- cist into a sketch. The germ of the idea was that the assistant to the celebrity is always more important than the celebrity in Hollywood. The assistant has the keys to the kingdom. If you want to talk to the famous person, you have to get through them first. (I made my editor work with my assistant on this book. I've never even spoken to her!) I didn't know how to frame the sketch or who I was going to play yet—publicist, agent? I finally landed on personal assistant. Then I needed a setting. I decided on a waiting room of an office where the assistant would be alone with the people waiting to meet a "very important person," and where he could privately pull his power trip. I didn't know who to make the star but I thought it was funnier to make them someone less obvious. For some reason I chose Dick Clark . . . and I still don't know why. I must have just seen him on *New Year's Rockin' Eve* or some bullshit that year and decided that he was a guy not as powerful as say, Jeffrey Katzenberg or some studio head, so it would be that much more frustrating if his assistant was talking down to someone.

This is the week I made my move to do my own sketch, writing myself into the lead. To give myself an even better shot, I decided to try to use the musical guest. David Bowie was appearing on the show that week with his band Tin Machine. I knew Bowie had acted before and I figured he'd be perfect because . . . well, he's DAVID BOWIE and therefore unbelievably famous. It would be a hilarious scenario if Bowie couldn't get in to see Dick Clark because of some asshole assistant. I wrote something up where David Bowie comes into the office and I, as the receptionist, stop him and make him explain to me who he is, why I should know him, list his credits . . . and ultimately not let him in. I would even make him sing. I typed this up (well, the typing girls did) and gave it to the talent department and they told me, "We will try to get this to David Bowie . . ." And I waited. And waited. The next day I came in and there was a lone message in my tiny little mailbox written on yellow NBC letterhead that said, "You missed a call from: David Bowie." My heart stopped. I missed a call from my musical hero. The return number was a Boston hotel with a fake name.

I remember I didn't call him until I was alone in my apartment and I had all my balls up. I couldn't do it in the office for fear of saying the wrong thing and having Farley or Sandler bust my chops or, worse yet, interrupt me. I nervously poked at the keys on the old-school push-button phone in my house (beep . . . boop . . .

beep beep . . .). I asked for his room and . . . David Bowie answered. I hadn't planned what to say. I was just winging it. Luckily, he was very nice. "David, I read your sketch, it's hilarious. I have to do this." I got an instant shot of adrenaline. He said, "I come back tomorrow so let's rehearse this and get it going." "Great! This will be really fun!" In my head I am thinking, I can't believe I am going to have a sketch, that I wrote, on *Saturday Night Live* WITH DAVID BOWIE. Then came the bombshell. "Just one thing . . . I want to play the receptionist, so who do we get to play me?" My heart stopped . . . Oh fuck, what? . . . Wait . . . what? Shit, what was I going to do? I was hoping to get a sketch on that I felt could help me finally gain some footing. What do I do? I can get a sketch on right now and gain some ground at work or keep waiting and try to get it going with a future host. I took the latter. I explained to DAVID BOWIE that the receptionist was a character I wanted to own, like Wayne from *Wayne's World*, and that I wanted to build him over multiple shows—and therefore I couldn't just hand it over. He then said, "Well, it's not fun playing myself." I could tell he was a bit annoyed, and I knew he was when he told me he had to go and hung up the phone. I was stunned. I couldn't believe that I had been able to talk to David Bowie, and then within four minutes piss him off enough to hang up so fast. And so much for my sketch idea. I spent another week getting paid by *SNL* for doing jack shit, basically. But this is life in the big city, like my dad had told me. (This was rich, of course, coming from the same guy who had skipped town all those years ago on my mom. It is hard to take advice from a guy who can't handle life in a small city.)

With the receptionist sketch already written, I just needed someone to plug into it. The next week's musical guest was M. C. Hammer, so I decided to roll the dice with him. To be honest, he wasn't exactly who I had in mind, but he was very famous at the time, so it made some sense. I reworked it from the David Bowie setup, but there were the same basic jokes—the receptionist (me) was to embarrass the star by asking them to recite their résumé, act out scenes from movies, and sing their songs or whatever to jog my memory. These are all things that actually happen in Los Angeles, and as such, the sketch got big laughs at read-through. I was so close to the finish line. The sketch just had to play well in front of the audience at dress, and then it would make the cut to get on air.

I found out between dress and air that the sketch did make the cut, but it would be the last sketch of the show, at five minutes to 1 A.M. I couldn't have cared less. I didn't bother calling anyone at home to say stay up, because the issue with the "5 to 1" sketch is that the show expands or contracts according to how big the laughs are with a particular audience. If the crowd is great and the other sketches get major laughs, the final sketch of the night usually gets cut during the show. That is why that last sketch is also referred to as "cut bait" (lingo!). You never want your sketch to be referred to as cut bait. Well, luck was on my side. We made it on. Hammer was great and the sketch made an impact. We got laughs. This was the days before Twitter and Instagram so it was literally word of mouth. I got good feedback from friends and people I ran into, but as Lorne says, that kind of thing doesn't count. One of the many wise things Lorne tells each cast member early on is that "people will tell you you're the funniest person on the show. You're not." That kind of cold reality really takes your legs out from under you right out of the gate, even though it is completely true.

But even Lorne gave good feedback on the sketch. I heard from other writers and cast members. I felt so relieved to finally have a sketch under my belt that worked. I finally felt like I was part of the show and not just an observer. Naturally I wanted to do that sketch again, as soon as possible. But I had to give it a little breathing room.

Five weeks later, Roseanne Barr was hosting, and lucky for me she was game. Phil Hartman also joined her, playing Jesus, and the one-two punch of those two made the sketch crush pretty well in read-through. The sketch did so well at dress rehearsal that it got moved to the very first sketch after the monologue, the point in the show when there are the most viewers. Anything on before Weekend Update is solid because that's when we have a big tune-out problem. This was my best week on the show to that point. The sketch got better every time it ran. It did so great on air that I felt like I might actually spend the summer not worried about getting fired.

Well, that feeling didn't last long. By the end of my third year, I was again on the chopping block. Nothing I did after my second receptionist sketch landed on air. The stress was getting to me. My neck hurt, my jaw hurt from grinding my teeth at night. I wasn't sleeping well and was very thin because of my lousy diet of pizza and pussy. (I say pussy because it sounds funny but I wasn't getting any action. Stressed writers/barely performers aren't as sexy as they sound.) I'm pretty sure I didn't eat a single vegetable my entire *Saturday Night Live* career and I'm sure I had some level of malnourishment. My hair turned brown from being in New York for so long. I never knew my hair could be anything but really blond and fluffy, in that beautiful Farrah Fawcett way I had always known. I had spent my whole life in the sunshine of Arizona and then L.A. But six months out of the year in dreary, sunless, creaky midtown Manhattan buildings made my blond hair brown. It sounds like a Crystal Gayle song, but it's true.

I wondered if I should just pack it in. This was too fucking brutal.

CHAPTER TWELVE

SNL 1992-1993

The summer of 1992, I was still on thin ice. All my pals were killing it. Schneider had scored with the Copy Guy skit. Adam was creating one awesome character after another. Chris was just on fuego. We were all doing gigs to make extra cash, but that year, Adam's road price shot through the roof. Your road price was another way to know how you were doing on *SNL*. Adam, Rob, and I had always made the same price for stand-up gigs the first year we were all together on the show. But then Adam's started to creep up on mine. Eventually he started to get double my rate. We would still go out on the road together but he now closed the shows. Adam was clearly the bigger draw. It was slightly humiliating, but I chose to look at it from the perspective that I had never made so much money on the road before in my life. I knew there were tons of comics out there who made a lot less than I was making. I was fucking lucky.

But it's hard to keep that attitude while you are on *Saturday Night Live*. It is very much a culture of comparison—you look at what your peers have and what you have and you are constantly doing the math to see who is on top. It is almost impossible to avoid, but you have to try if you want to stay sane. (Take my advice, young *SNL* wannabes.) I'm just as competitive as the next guy, but if you handle competition like a dick, you'll end up ruining your career and your friendships. At the time, though, it was a bitter pill to watch my pals doing so well while I was having such a hard time. I can admit that.

By late summer, I still didn't know if I was going to be invited back to the show. The only thing I'd done of note the previous season had been my receptionist sketch, but that didn't seem like enough to get me picked up. That and "being fun around the office" was about all I had going for me. And even that I wasn't always sure about. Chris, Rob, Adam, they had already gotten their calls. Once again I had to sweat it out longer than anyone. At some point in early August, one of my managers talked to Lorne and told me, "He's bringing you back. But you really have to work hard. And, you're still going to be a writer/feature player." This was disappointing to me. I was now the only chump in my "class" left slaving away at those rewrite meetings. Sandler was now a full cast member, and Rob, and Farley had been one basically since the day he started (deservedly so). What this also meant was that none of the new writers would feel any responsibility to put me into their sketches. Why would they? I had been treading water with minimal talent for a long time and didn't know how long it was gonna last.

The host for our first show that season was Nicolas Cage. I came out swinging hard . . . and whiffed three times. I got nothing on the show at all, so I was off to my typical strong start of being invisible. (This helped me later when I played the Invisible Man in *Hotel Transylvania*. I drew from my real feelings.) Next up was Tim Robbins, and this show was a very important and memorable one for me for several reasons. The first, and most important, reason is that it was the show where I finally saved my ass on *SNL*. I was sitting at the writers' table on Monday, bored as usual. I was reading *People* magazine out loud and basically shitting on every celebrity featured. Bob Odenkirk, bless his heart, was sitting near me and said, "You have to write that up." And so the Hollywood Minute sketch was born. During that read-through, Lorne said to me, "You've found your voice." And that was the best fucking thing I could possibly hear. I could tell by the way he said it that he was happy, and that I was actively saving my job in the process. The first Hollywood Minute bit went off without a hitch. The audience bought into it right away. A young loser nobody from Arizona, taking out major celebrities at the knees—well, it just clicked from the first burn. A new segment had been born for me, one that would become my best move at that place. This was a time when there was only *People* magazine. It was always fawning over these guys and no one was saying what people really thought. That was my great timing award, because after that came *Entertainment Weekly* and blogs where everyone got super-snarky on celebs. So I got lucky there.

But that show is also memorable for other, more unfortunate reasons. You see, Tim Robbins is a pretty political guy. He was hosting *SNL* and he wanted to make a statement. In the Monday meeting he explained to us: "I want to go after everybody in my monologue . . . all these big corporations, even GE." (As in General Electric, then NBC's parent company.) Everyone sort of nodded along and pretended that we thought that was hilarious, and then we went about our business writing sketches that did not shit on GE. Well, during his monologue on Saturday night, Tim Robbins went for it. He made some political statements. He made some jokes. I recall him quietly singing the GE ad slogan but changing the last bit to "GE, we bring good things to . . . death." The cast and the audience awkwardly laughed because honestly, it was more of a comment than a joke. But he had done what he set out to do and he was happy, I guess.

I think he was hoping some of the media would pick up on his statement and run with it, which may have happened . . . EEEEEEEEXCEEEPPPPPT . . . about twenty minutes later, Sinéad O'Connor came on to sing one of her dopey songs. (If it wasn't "Nothing Compares 2 U," I wasn't listening.) I remember I was standing behind Lorne watching the monitor and sort of basking in the glory of my Hollywood Minute sketch doing well, waiting for him to put his arm around my shoulders and say, "Good job, son." And while I was there quietly begging for a Snausage from Lorne, I saw something odd on the screen. At the end of her snoozer tune, Sinéad held up a picture of Pope John Paul and said, "Fight the real enemy," and ripped it up into ten pieces. The room fell silent.

"Oh snap . . . no she di-int." (I wish I made that phrase up, because that moment was the perfect place to bust it out.) I wondered the same thing everyone else on the cast probably did: *Is this part of the show?* And then she dropped the pieces on the stage and nervously scurried away. The crowd was dead silent. It's the first time in *SNL* musical history that the guest did not get applause after their song. No one knew what the fuck was going on. Lorne turned back to me after sipping his glass of Amstel Light, shrugged his shoulders, and said, "Irish." I had to laugh. During the commercial, I walked out to the stage, looked down at what was left of the pope there on the floor, and grabbed a piece. As I stuffed it in my pocket I thought, This will be a nice memento if anyone ever remembers this happening.

Cut to the next day. This shit is world news. People are freaking the fuck out. I don't know much about religion. It wasn't part of our family culture at all. My mom didn't have much time for church. She had to work and fight my dad for child support that never came. So I didn't really get what the big deal was. All I knew was that Sinéad O'Connor was kind of sexy when she got to the studio that week, and I sort of flirted with her. Then I decided that I wouldn't try to sleep with her since she was now a worldwide pariah, which is a major boner killer.

That Sunday night while I was doing my piles of laundry in the basement of my dogshit apartment building, I watched *Inside Edition*. As my flannel shirts were drying, there was Deborah Norville yammering on about *Saturday Night Live*. I pushed my two-foot stack of quarters to the side to get a better look, and saw that they were actually reporting on how Sinéad O'Connor had ripped up a picture of the pope on camera! Then they put the torn pieces back together to make the photo whole again. Well, almost whole . . . because there was one piece missing. My eyes slowly drifted over past the laundry machine quarters to that little slice of pope I had snagged the night before. I held it up to the television screen, and it fit perfectly. *Inside Edition* clearly had the ACTUAL photo that this Sinéad chick had shredded!! How did that happen?? I had told Adam and a few others that night that I had taken a little piece of the pope pic with me, and sure enough the next day I got hauled into *SNL* producer Kenny Aymong's office. (I love Kenny Aymong. He was always very cool to me during my *SNL* years. Even when I was a nobody, which was most of my time there.) Kenny sat me down with two security guards and said, "You might have something that belongs to us." And, ever the smart-ass, I popped back with, "Oh, I don't think so unless you're talking about a pile of bad sketches that never got on the air." I chuckled. No one else did. One of the security guys then said, "Do you have a piece of the pope picture?" And I said, "Oh that . . . uh yeah, I guess I do. Who ratted me out?" (I still thought the situation was funny. I was clearly not reading the room very well.) Then the security guard asked, "Do you have it with you?" Of course I did, because I wanted to show off and talk about anything but Joe Pesci sketch ideas that day. It quickly became clear to me that I needed to hand that piece of the pope over, and quick. These security dudes weren't messing around.

I learned soon after that a member of the crew had stolen the ripped-up photo off the floor and sold it to *Inside Edition* for ten thousand dollars. He was fired, but security thought that I might be in on it. Kenny knew I wasn't, but he had to follow protocol. We laughed about it later, even though we agreed I could have used part of that 10K. The rest of the season I peppered in a few Hollywood Minutes sketches, and I felt I was officially on the radar. It took me way too long, let's be honest, but by midseason I had the audacity to believe that I might be able to enjoy summer without worrying about getting canned. We had a solid lineup of hosts that year, and ratings were good. I remember during February sweeps the musical guests were Bon Jovi, Madonna, Mick Jagger, Paul McCartney, and Sting. That's a pretty solid lineup. But in the nineteenth show of the year, I was part of the most memorable sketch of my *SNL* career.

I had heard about the Motivational Speaker character here and there throughout the year. Farley and Bob Odenkirk used to talk about it a lot in the office. They discussed that and a sketch called Whale Boy—two ideas that they had worked up at Second City and were trying to bring to *SNL*. Well, the week that Christina Applegate was the host was the week that they decided to put it out there, with Chris in the lead. (I almost said "and the rest is history" but it's too corny, even though it's kind of true.) Christina and I were cast as the two kids the speaker had been brought in to motivate. Phil Hartman played our nerdy dad, clearly at his wits' end with his troublemaker kids and making a last-ditch effort. This was the most tailor-made Chris Farley sketch ever, a fastball right down the middle that he could knock out of the park. It was physical, it was hilarious, and with his scratchy-hoarse voice, Chris made it even funnier. He slicked his hair back after seeing Christian Slater do it when he hosted the year before. He had already started wearing these massive Dan Aykroyd–style reading glasses every day, so those became part of the costume. It all came together with that horrible plaid blazer. Matt Foley was born. This was one of those bits where everybody on the floor was laughing every rehearsal. It was pretty bulletproof. There was no way it could go south because the more Chris stumbled, stammered, and squinted at the cue cards, the funnier it was.

When we did it on the show, we were all prepped not to laugh. These were the days before Fallon and Horatio Sanz were losing their shit a lot on air. Lorne did not like laughing in sketches during our era. There was a very strict rule for us that we were not *The Carol Burnett Show* and must stay in character at all times. Of course, Chris didn't give a shit about those rules and did his best to make Adam or me laugh in every single sketch we were in with him. He felt like it was victory if he broke us, which it was. During some sketches, he would get close enough to me that he could headbutt me and throw me off (it worked every time). Other times, he would be facing me and cross his eyes, cracking me up with something the audience couldn't see. Or he would overly ham up a line in a way he had never done in rehearsals, and totally throw me off. It is now very well known that Christina and I totally lost it during this sketch. The thing that set me off was Chris twisting back and forth on his belt like Chubby Checker. He looked like an idiot, and it caught me off guard. Then he did the running motion and that was it. Once I started to crack, he knew he could come in for the kill and he did. Christina and I didn't have a chance. *Rolling Stone* called this the best sketch of all time and while I'm not sure that's true (because there are too many to pick from), Matt Foley is definitely one of the greatest characters ever on *Saturday Night Live*.

I was very lucky that I had a front-row seat for it, and it is one of my favorite memories of Chris. We did Motivational Speaker a few more times and the head writers were cool enough to always put me in it. My second favorite one is where he tries to speak Spanish and basically reads it phonetically off cue cards. (SAY YAMMA SOY ME HOMBRE . . .) The whole sketch was hysterical to me because in rehearsal I kept laughing and yelling, "Chris, what the fuck are you doing? Pretend we're in the sketch with you." Then he would laugh and go, "Shut up, David." That pretty much turned into "Shut up, Richard" in *Tommy Boy* because he said it so much.

During this season, Chris dated one of Lorne's assistants. She was this sweet, preppy blond girl we all thought was super-cute and fun. Chris and Erin dated on and off for a while but eventually called it quits—for a myriad of reasons that she never really told me. But she did once tell me that she went back to Wisconsin with Chris and stayed at his childhood home with him. She was totally traumatized by dinner, which consisted of his dad bringing in a big platter of steaks and everyone just going at them like a bunch of crazed wolverines. Then Chris's mom carried around the "yuck bag" and each man would spit his bones into it. I busted Chris's balls about the yuck bag forever, and how horrifying it must have been for this sheltered, waspy East Coast girl to see the Farley family eat dinner, with all the booze and bones flying.

A few weeks after they broke up, word got around that Erin

was dating someone else. Then we heard who the new guy was, and we decided not to tell Chris right away. But one day he confronted me and Sandler. "I hear Erin's got some new boy toy. Did you hear about this shit?" And we said, "Um, yeah." And he goes, "Well, he might be better looking than me but he's not funnier, he's not richer, and he's sure as fuck not more famous." And we stared at Chris for a few seconds in silence. Finally, I had to break it to him. "We've got some bad news . . . you're oh for three, pal. She's dating Steve Martin." Crickets . . . then, "Ah fuck!!!!"

CHAPTER THIRTEEN
SNL 1993-1994

For the 1993–94 season, I was finally a full cast member. True to my *SNL* employment pattern, I didn't learn this news until the very end of the summer, after another long, hot season of sweating bullets waiting to be fired. I was excited to finally have taken the next step, but to find out so late was a bit embarrassing. I was bummed this year because Chris Rock was gone. By this point we had become really tight. But to be honest, he was frustrated, and *Saturday Night Live* was never the perfect place for him. So he left the show and went back to his stand-up roots. Two years later, in 1996, he released the unbelievable stand-up special *Bring the Pain* and reminded everyone what all the fuss was about.

He deserved that and busted his ass to do it. We were all stoked it paid off huge for him. He was back on top.

I, on the other hand, was busy finding my fourth apartment on the Upper West Side and writing sketches about working at the Gap. Remember that little doozy? I had been home in Arizona once, shopping at the Gap for some of their exceptional ring-neck T-shirts when I overheard two chicks folding clothes. I sat there listening to one tell the other something along the lines of, "You're folding those cable crews wrong." "I know, I missed the folding meeting." "Oh my God, you're going to get so busted," and back and forth. The girls themselves even laughed at how stupid their conversation was. It gave me the idea of a sketch of guys working at the Gap and having these asinine conversations. Then I thought it would be even funnier if we dressed in drag and played it as girls. Now, this wound up being a bit sticky because there were not enough parts for girls on the show already, and this sketch had parts for four girls being taken up by guys. I decided not to worry about that and to look out for numero uno because, according to my calculations, I was on air less than most of the girls anyway. I had to remember the old "nobody said life was fair" motto. The other benefit of this sketch was that it gave me a reason to hang out with Farley, Sandler, and Schneider all week. That made coming to work a lot more fun.

The first host that season was Charles Barkley, and he was up for playing a girl with long dreadlocks, and I wrote the sketch so that we had a girl-girl hookup at a keg party during a game of Truth or Dare. (Edgy!) I also wrote a part of the sketch that had the Gap girls going to a Nirvana concert, and having the band hit on them backstage. It was so fucking stupid, but we had the balls to ask Nirvana to actually do it. (On a side note: I'm still in shock that I met Kurt Cobain. He was one of the most memorable, interesting people who came through that show. I sat down with the band at dinner break once and they were all very cool. I some-times feel I have a kinship with Dave Grohl, because both of the guys we were very close to got very famous quickly and then died, and we stuck around to field questions about them for the rest of our lives. It is an honor, but not an easy one sometimes.)

The day before we were set to film the backstage segment, we heard from the music department that Nirvana was not going to do the sketch. I was all fired up, so bummed that my brilliant sketch was in jeopardy. "Why not?" I asked. "We didn't ask them." I stood there in shock. "Why didn't you?" "Maybe because the sketch shows the band trying to date-rape you and Adam backstage and maybe their managers wouldn't think that was super-appropriate." Sheepishly, I said, "Oh yeah, I guess I can see that." But I still wouldn't give up. I liked the idea of Adam and me getting drunk and making our way backstage at a concert, and having Adam run out moments later screaming, "He grabbed my boob!" and me, "Where's my scrunchie? Just run!" with our shirts half off. There was no way I was throwing away this award-winning scene.

So we called the band Skid Row and they were more than happy to come in from New Jersey and help us out. Lead singer Sebastian Bach and guitarist Rachel Bolan came over and played it perfectly, and I'm sure Nirvana were kicking themselves when they saw this amazing piece of comedy on air. The Skid Row guys were nuts. When they were on the show Sebastian Bach yelled, "We are live, motherfucker!" at the end of his song, which I thought was funny. Especially on a show called *Saturday Night Live*. No one broke the rules there, but Sebastian Bach just didn't give a fuck. It wasn't like they were Guns N' Roses or the Stones. They were a solid band with two good songs at the time. I'm not even sure the swearing went out on the air; I thought it did but I didn't hear anything about it afterward. The other thing Bach did that was pure insanity was wear a T-shirt during the "good nights" that had a Raid can on it with dead bugs around it. Everyone had seen the ad that said, "Raid: kills bugs dead." As he was waving good night, I looked closer and realized much to my shock that it didn't say that . . . it said, "AIDS: kills fags dead." I was like, "Ummm." Wearing that shirt today would get you kicked out of show business immediately; in fact, you should just see yourself out if you wore something like that. But at the time, there wasn't much of a controversy over that shirt, which seems shocking. I'm sure today Sebastian regrets wearing it. Thank God that's one style from the nineties that hasn't resurfaced at Urban Outfitters.

After the first Gap Girls sketch went well, I was all gung-ho to come up with another one, and one of them from this season ranks in the top five most memorable sketches I appeared in during my *SNL* run. (The first Motivational Speaker sketch is the top, but I take zero credit for how great that one is. Anybody could have played my part.) There was a Gap Girls sketch we did when Sara Gilbert was the host. I decided to leave the date rape out of this one. Farley made this one memorable, as he did for so many sketches, but at least I got to write what he said. The idea this time around was that the Gap Girls were on break in the mall food court, and they get in a heated argument with the girls from Donut Hut. Chris, Adam, and I were the Gap Girls again, and Schneider and Sara Gilbert played the Donut Hut chicks. Clearly there was a tense rivalry between these two factions, one that hadn't been seen since the Jets and the Sharks in *West Side Story*. It started out with us discussing current events and getting almost everything wrong, from calling carpal tunnel syndrome *carpet* tunnel syndrome to discussing the trial of the "Menenenedez" brothers. We didn't know what the fuck we were talking about. Then there came the infamous fries joke, which was inspired by the fact that Chris always ate the fries off my plate whenever we were in a restaurant together. If you watch closely, you can see me mouthing everyone's lines as the sketch goes on. This happens a lot when you write sketches—you just want the jokes to work perfectly and I was desperate for Chris not to fuck up the "LAY OFF ME I'M STARVING" line because I wanted it to work so badly. The real kick was the quiet "Diet starts Monday" right after. I saw that quote on a meme recently, and I was so happy that something I scribbled twenty years ago on a wrinkled legal pad at a crummy wooden desk at four in the morning was still funny to someone today.

After that the girls enter from Donut Hut and Sara says, "Oh, there's the Gap girls and they're eating again, what a surprise." They continue to make fun of me because I'm dating a loser who doesn't really like me. Sample: Adam: "He's so mean to you, doesn't he always tell you, you look like you slept on your face?" And I say, "Yeah, but he's just really honest." Adam: "Well, what about when you reminded him that he owes you $600 and he punched you in the neck?" Me: "Well, he's just really sensitive. He's a Cancer." There was another throwaway joke we put in to see if the audience would get it—a time lapse. When there is a time lapse in a sketch, the graphics department just puts up an exterior photo, in this case of the mall, with the words "Four days later" on the bottom. Obviously they come back to us just still sitting there ten seconds later. So I added, "Isn't it funny that we are all wearing the same outfits from four days ago?" And then Adam says, "No, we're not." And I go, "Trust me, we are." People think I made that up that night but it was planned, I'm sad to say. I made up that joke at rehearsal and we decided to keep it in. The last question I get about that sketch is about how at the very end we say, "The Donut Hut girls are always OTR!" Some people have asked me what that meant. In Arizona when girls were bitchy we said they were "on the rag." And so I thought everyone knew what OTR meant. Apparently, it's not universal. But that's what I get for being from Scottsdale.

Another favorite that year was yet another sketch that involved me playing a smart-ass. (Do you see a theme?) It was on the show that Helen Hunt hosted, and we played rude asshole flight attendants. Fred Wolf, one of the longtime great writers on the show, had an idea about two sweet, blond, all-American flight attendants standing at the door as everyone exits . . . and saying the now infamous "Buh-Bye" to everyone as they leave. The "Buh-Bye" is laced with some venom, so that what you really hear is "get the hell out of here," which you know is what flight attendants are thinking after hours of taking care of a hundred demanding assholes on an airplane. (That's got to be one of the worst jobs. Especially when I'm flying!)

This sketch had a great hook and was perfect for Helen Hunt and me. The audience related to it and responded so well because we've all seen those flight attendants in our own lives. Sometimes you notice something in the world that seems funny to you. This angle of escalating the "Buh-Bye" more and more was just funny to me. Fred and I were good buddies, and we wrote the sketch together. It did well at read-through and we laughed a ton during rehearsals because the sketch just got funnier and funnier as it went on. There was the very end, when Sandler wanted to beat me up, and I just kept yelling "Buh-Bye" at him like a tough guy, or how we replaced the lyrics of songs from the seventies with "Buh-Bye." "Awww Buh-*Bye*!" to the tune of "Freak Out" and "Do the Buh-Bye" instead of "Do the Hustle." He called the airline TBA for Total Bastard Air—I was slightly surprised that got through Standards and Practices.

The sketch really came together and did well on the air but you never really know what's going to resonate. Without Twitter, Facebook, and Instagram you couldn't really get a feel for what people liked. You just had to go by what you heard from your friends and hopefully what Lorne heard from his Upper East Side pals. But I got on a plane the next day to head back to Los Angeles for a two-week break and all the flight attendants started "Buh-Bye" the minute I walked on. For probably the next ten years I have had someone say "Buh-Bye" to me at least once a day. American Airlines even used the sketch in their training seminars to show the perception of flight attendants, and how it needs to be changed for the better. Recently, when I was leaving Burger King (I like to eat healthy!) there were stickers on the door that said "Buh-Bye" in huge letters. Watching *SNL* as a kid, there were always those sketches, those catchphrases that became part of popular culture. When I got on the show, I wanted desperately to be a part of one of those. All I wanted to have accomplished when I left the show was to have been in a sketch and said a line that people repeated. I think that was the closest I came to that. After the receptionist, I got a lot of "Annnnnddddddd Youuuuuuu Arrrrrrrre?" But "Buh-Bye" remains the most repeatable and remembered.

What I also learned from that sketch was that people like what they like. We did that sketch once that season, and I heard about it for five years. Dana and Mike did Wayne's World at least twenty-five times, and it was a massive hit and created a million catchphrases. But my point is that there was something about that one sketch that people latched on to and it became a "thing." We even tried "Buh-Bye" one more time the following season and it just didn't have the same vibe to it. Today no one remembers that one, but everyone remembers the first one . . .

Soon Adam and Chris were about to go and take over Hollywood. I wasn't ready to leave yet, having just been made a full cast member, so I stayed another year. Lorne gave me a weekly five-minute segment called "Spade in America," during which I could do whatever I wanted. I enjoyed that, but I sort of felt like I was back on the wall outside the high school cafeteria. I was the guy who had graduated but couldn't quite get a life. Most of my squad was gone and now it was Will Ferrell, Molly Shannon, and Cheri

Oteri's turn to take over. I liked Will a lot because I thought he was hilarious. I invited him to lunch one week. Like a selfish prick, I ate before he got there. He was so surprised that I had done that, and I felt like the biggest asshole alive. Even though it was and is something I do to my friends all the time, this was symbolic. My time was done. I should have just moved on and let those guys have at it. I was sort of in the way now.

There is one bit from that year that I do want to discuss. It was a field bit that involved Sean Penn and a tattoo. At this point, I didn't know Sean Penn at all, but I had heard talking at a party about learning to do tattoos on potatoes or pig ears. I don't know how this stuck in my head, or if it is even true, but a week later I was desperate for an idea for the show (again) and read that Penn was in town for Letterman that week. So I had the brilliant idea to ask him to come in and give me a tattoo. (Brought to you by www.dumbideas.com.) So I asked Lovitz for his number. Lovitz made me promise I wouldn't tell Sean Penn where I got his number. I left Sean a message telling him who I was, and asked if he would give me a tattoo while he was in town. He shockingly called me back a little later and said, "Sure, let's do it." He didn't seem too nervous about possibly ruining my upper arm for the rest of my life.

So now I had to a) go through with this and b) find a tattoo I liked. I found a tat based on one that Steven Tyler had on his arm that I thought was cool. I had it all drawn up and I was ready to go. For legal reasons, we had to meet outside of Manhattan, so I had the show send a car for Sean. For hours I was in a grubby little tattoo parlor with my film crew waiting for a guy I don't know to come destroy my beautiful epidermis . . . actually to finish the job the Arizona sun started. The owner was a big, burly dude who actually knew Sean, and two other Hells Angels were there to meet him for some reason. This was not my typical scene. I was a squirrely punk from Scottsdale who was more comfortable sitting

in the shallow end of an empty pool with a few other skaters waiting to drop into the deep end. So I sat there awkwardly trying to
jabber with these shady characters about feathering hair techniques
or anything I could think of. At this point, Sean was two hours
late. My driver got lost and then reported that Sean wanted some
vodka, so they pulled over.

To kill time I filmed the owner giving me a tour of his fine
establishment and me wisecracking about different tattoos, none
of which made him even crack a smile. Sean finally rolled in, what
felt like five hours later, slightly buzzed, but super-nice and ready to
go. I showed him the tattoo sketch I had picked and as he looked at
it curiously the owner said, "There's no way he can do this one. It's
too complicated." So I asked, "What could he pull off?" We ended
up going through the comics section of the newspaper, and the one
that was decided on was Calvin from *Calvin and Hobbes*. As much
as I thought this was a mildly amusing comic, I definitely did not
want to have that drawing on my arm for the rest of my life, but the
show must go on.

Sean started doing the tattoo while I interviewed him about
his career and world events. I was trying to make him laugh over
the buzzing noise and the pain. Not a great idea. "You know when
I laugh, I'm even worse at this," he said, which was not reassuring
since he wasn't so good when he wasn't laughing. At this point I
decided I didn't care. I was already going to be maimed for life.
I just wanted a good bit out of all of this. When we were in the
middle of the interview, I hit him with one of my meanest jokes.
It was around the time Sandra Bullock was starring in the cyber-
thriller *The Net*. So after a few dumb questions about his career I
say, "By the way, did you see the talking pig movie?" And he shook
his head no, focusing on my pale arm. I continued, "Oh you didn't
see *The Net*?" And he took a beat and smiled and said something to
the effect of, "Oh, that's fucked up." Looking back, maybe it was

too rude to kick America's sweetheart Sandra Bullock in the balls because for one movie she was maybe five pounds overweight, but I had to get it in there and it fucking cracked me up for some reason. Just because it was so shitty and so out of left field. Anyway, I got back to the show and played the bit and to this day, I don't think people really thought it was a legit tattoo. But if you ever see me on the beach looking like a moron flexing with Calvin on one of my mega guns, you'll see Sean's handiwork for yourself.

BEING VALUABLE

want to take an opportunity to say a few words here about Rob Schneider. I've written a lot about him in this book. It is probably obvious that we were friendly rivals. Sometimes not friendly. Sometimes the rivalry only went one way—as in I saw him as a rival while he was riding high. I don't want people reading this to think that there is bad blood between us. Rob and I have many years of being in the trenches together, and all those shared experiences have given me some perspective on things. Robert Smigel, I think it was, said once during a period on *SNL* when there was a chance that Rob would be fired, that he wouldn't because Rob was "valuable." The phrase was something along the lines of "We shouldn't get rid of him, he's valuable." This was a time when Rob was really rubbing folks the wrong way on the show. It wasn't just me. But when I heard that, I thought that "valuable" was a really interesting word choice. I didn't get what that even meant in that context. What I thought was, Here's a guy who can get Phil Hartman to throw him against the wall in anger. Here's a guy who has Jack Handy grousing about him. This guy is annoying two of the nicest people in the building. And yet, he's valuable? That really stuck with me. I figured out later it meant because he is good at his job. At the end of the day, he's a good writer. He's a good performer. And he could add funny ideas and lines to existing sketches.

I wanted to be valuable. I was jealous of that. He brought more positive than negative to the table. So I saw that and realized that in Hollywood, it was just a blip on the radar. The big examples are huge stars and how much shit they can get away with, versus how much money they're bringing in or how much they bring to a project. You see it all over now. You can get drunk at work if you're doing a show that is making money. You can do everything wrong like Charlie Sheen, but if you get your fucking lines right and someone makes money, people give you a pass. (Sheen is a bad example because he got shitcanned. BUT then he jumped on another show and made someone else a ton of cash. And he didn't change his tune at all.) I try not to be a total disaster at work, but I do try to be valuable. I try to bring whatever I can to the table. I want whatever project I'm on to do well.

It's all very tricky now. It was really tricky back then. I sound like I'm slamming Rob, but actually, I'm slamming myself. I had a lot I needed to learn back then. We all did.

Here's what I learned from *SNL*. When people are better than you don't be jealous. Respect it and use it to drive yourself to be better. I got in stand-up on a whim but once I made the choice I wanted to be great at it. So many people at the show were so much better than me and I couldn't deal with it at first. It takes a lot to be great and I was surrounded by it. I felt like a good high school player that got moved up to the pros. But running with people better than you always makes you faster and that's what I got from *SNL*. It made a lazy guy work harder than I ever wanted to.

The good news is that Rob and I are still buddies. We started hanging out again when we were making the movie *The Benchwarmers*. It's all good. We were all just young and scratching to be famous and broke a few eggs back then.

CHAPTER FOURTEEN

EDDIE MURPHY AND ME

My infamous run-in with Eddie Murphy has been discussed and repeated so many times over the years, by so many people, that I'm sort of done with it. But I feel like I should put it down in print one final time, to sort of put the bow on it and move on. That way, when the aliens come looking for some mildly amusing anecdotes to take back to their planet when they blow ours to smithereens, this one will be primed and ready to go.

When I finally came up with my Hollywood Minute sketch, as previously recounted in great (and probably excruciatingly boring) detail, it was a huge relief to me. I needed something to stick. Things were so dire for me then that whenever I saw Adam Sandler in his office tuning his guitar I'd just crumple up whatever I was writing, go out for pizza, and stick a gun in my mouth between bites. Because he always killed.

The first joke I used on Hollywood Minute went along with a photo of Michael Bolton. The line went "Hey, Michael Bolton, your hair is really long in the back, but guess what? We all know what's happening on top. It's called Rogaine, look into it." Then came "I know you've sold eight million albums but guess what? I don't know anyone that has one!" Laughs all around. I did "the min" (gross term for it that I never actually called it) again two weeks later, and then as often as I could despite everyone probably rolling their eyes whenever I brought it to the table.

The bit was working and now the cast and other writers were baiting me, daring me to go after certain people. Jim Downey was notorious for egging me on, and I was easily swayed by him because he was my boss, he is a great writer, and I was desperate to impress him in any way I could. Plus I needed attention. (Barf.) As time went on, I hit some peeps pretty hard, but I only did so if I felt they deserved it. It's a fine line between clever and just mean. I did cross it a few times, but I went for laughs. Some of my favorite jokes back then were ripping on Downtown Julie Brown after she had left MTV (*Wubba wubba wubba, my career's in trubba trubba trubba*), and M. C. Hammer (*Do do do doot do doot do dooot, it's over*). I went for Jim Carrey once, and I can say it was too soon—people loved him too much. I loved him, too, frankly, but this was a case of writers egging me on, daring me to go after him. I did the joke at dress rehearsal, but I got so many hisses that I pulled it. I liked it though: "Jim Carrey was hospitalized this week on the set of his movie after mixing over-the-top pills with play-it-too-big juice. It can be a deadly combo. He's fine now and quietly overacting at home." A lot of the time I was going after friends, friends who happened to be in the news, so it felt like an omission if I skipped the story. But in the case of Jim Carrey, I'm glad that joke didn't make it to air.

Now we come to the infamous Eddie Murphy Hollywood Minute. Here's the story, as I remember it. After this I swear I am never talking about this again. (Of course I will.) One week I was writing my dopey Hollywood Minute, my bread and butter and basically the only thing keeping me from going back out on the road doing shows at the Gut Busters in Omaha or working in the skateboard shop. I was sort of addicted to doing them because it was the only thing keeping me in front of the camera. So I'm sitting in my dumpy office and I realized that Eddie Murphy had put out two back-to-back flops. (By the way, there couldn't be a harsher word to hit your ear when you're an actor than *flop*. It's brutal. Short, harsh, and to the point. The past tense is even worse, as in "I heard your movie FUCKING FLOPPED!" So awful, and I should know. I've heard it a lot. That and *bombed*. But I hate *flop* more.) I think the two films were *Harlem Nights* and *Vampire in Brooklyn*. So, I casually write a joke about Eddie Murphy for my piece that week. You know the line. "Look, kids, a falling star! Quick, make a wish . . ."

The burn skims by on air, gets sort of a laugh mixed with an, "Ooo no you di-int" response, and I think nothing of it. Especially because it's buried in the middle of ten or twelve of these rapid-fire sizzles that come and go quickly.

So, on the following Monday at around 5 P.M. I was sitting in the writers' room reading the paper and waiting for the meeting with that week's host when an NBC page came into the room. He looked at me a little oddly and said, "Eddie Murphy is on the phone for you."

My heart stopped. WTF? "Um, seriously?" I squeaked.

"Yes, line two."

"Ummmmmmmmm. I'm not here, take a message."

She walked away. I could tell she was a bit starstruck (by him, not me) and curious as to why Eddie was calling me. Also curious as to why I wasn't sprinting to the phone. Meanwhile, I was quietly shitting diarrhea into my Dockers, out the window, and down Sixth Avenue, thinking, *Holy shit! Why is this famous motherfucker calling me? My spider senses are tingling. He has to be pissed! What do I say? I just did that joke about him. That has to be it!* In other words I was freaking the fuck out. I didn't know if I should call him back, or act like I didn't know he had called, or hide under Lorne's desk till this crazy storm blew over or what . . . I was starting to have an actual, official panic attack when . . .

RIIIIINNNGGGGGGG!!

The phone seven feet from me in the writers' room started ringing. One of the assistants picked it up.

"Writers' room . . . hang on . . . David, it's Eddie Murphy."

"Can't find me," I said casually, staring a hole through *People* magazine, pretending to read it, frozen in total, unmitigated fear. By now my heartbeat had picked up the pace a bit.

She hung up. I broke out of my trance and realized I needed to enlist Chris Rock. He covers all bases. He's my black friend, so any black-related problems go across his desk. He gets cc'd on everything. And he's Eddie's buddy, too, so he knows what I'm dealing with. He will have special insight, like when a movie brings in a real forensic criminologist to be a consultant. Rock knows what makes this guy tick. He could solve this. But before I could even get up to find Rock, I had a new problem.

RIIIIINNNGGGGGGG!!

HE'S CALLING AGAIN! WHAT. THE. FUCK.

"Eddie Murphy again . . ." the page said.

"I'm in a meeting," I lied.

"He says he knows you're not in a meeting, because it's five forty-five P.M. and the Monday host meeting is at six and it's never on time. He says call him back right now, or he's driving in from Brooklyn to talk to you in person."

I was staring at this page in disbelief. Why on God's green

earth was this superstar blowing me up three times in a row?? Didn't he have money to count or chicks to bang? (One day, twenty years later, someone had this very thought about me! Success!) Chris Rock then walked in and said, "You better call him; you don't want him coming down here. Don't forget, he's still a black guy."

No shit. I don't want this guy coming to have a talk with me. Even if he's famous. He scares me. I have no choice. So I take his number and asked Chris to get on the other phone to listen in and protect me.

I dialed . . .

My heart was pounding. I didn't want to do this, especially since I had zero game plan.

"Hello?"

A woman's voice answered! My heart leapt! Perhaps I had dialed the wrong number.

"Um, is Eddie there? It's . . . David Spade." I'm sure my voice cracked like Peter Brady in that *Brady Bunch* episode where he goes through pubie.

"Hang on," she said. Then, muffled, "It's him."

Stomach in knots, I heard, "Hello."

"Hey, Eddie, it's Spade."

(Dramatic pause. If this was a Lifetime movie we would definitely fade to commercial at this point.)

Now here comes Eddie . . . "David Spade, who the fuck do you think you are?!! Honestly? Who. The. Fuck. Going after ME?? You dumb motherfucker! I'm off-limits, don't you know that? You wouldn't have a job if it weren't for me. Talking shit about me??" Et cetera, et cetera, et cetera . . . on and on and on and making me feel like shit.

I barely spoke. I just stared at Rock in disbelief. It was so much worse than I had imagined. I wanted to apologize, explain the joke, anything, but nothing came out. Here was one of my favorite comedians of all time ripping me a new asshole. I had worshipped this dude for years, knew every line of his stand-up. And now he hated me. Like, really really hated me. The opposite of Sally Field. It was horrible. I didn't hate him. Of course not. He just got caught in friendly fire and my deep desire to make an impression on my bosses and keep my job. How pathetic. I took my beating and then he hung up.

Rock felt bad for me. He was caught in the middle. Old friend of Eddie's, new friend of mine. I said, "Rock, Eddie makes fun of Mr. T getting AIDS and a million other people in his HBO special. This joke was barely a flesh wound; it won't hurt him. WTF is he freaking out about? I'm nobody!" Rock tried to make me feel better but there was nothing he could do. He split back to his office. I kept thinking it wasn't fair.

But the truth was that when you are famous, you never want someone on a supposedly cool show to say you're not cool. Even if the person saying it is a nobody like me. Fame is so fragile and fleeting, and it can disappear for a million reasons. A jab like the one I had directed at Eddie can be the thing that starts to turn public opinion against someone. I try not to think of the casualties when I do rough jokes, but there are consequences sometimes. I know for a fact that I can't take it when it comes my way. It's horrible for all the same reasons. I've come to see Eddie's point on this one. Everybody in showbiz wants people to like them. That's how you get fans. But when you get reamed in a sketch or online or however, that shit staaaangs. And it can add up quickly. Then before you know it you're a punch line—just look at Vanilla Ice and five hundred million others. Eddie was mad. No one had dared go after him. And he wanted it to stop there.

After that incident I had some close encounters with Mr. Murphy. Once was at the opening of the Hard Rock Hotel in Las Vegas, when a bunch of celebs got invited to see a private Rolling Stones concert. (What a douche thing for me to mention in my book.) I brought one of my idiot buddies from high school. This was a fucking star-studded event. Brad Pitt to my right, Depp and DiCaprio at noon and six. There couldn't have been more celebs there and we were packed in like stardines. (Lolololololol, *stardines*, not *sardines*. Stay close.) I was having the time of my life when for some reason I glanced back to the row behind me. I think it was just to let those people know that I knew all the words to "Gimme Shelter." When who do I see down the row but Edward Murphy and Chris Rock? Oh fuck. My kryptonite was in the house. Suddenly . . . feeling . . . weak . . . I didn't want to get beat up in front of the Stones. It was going to be Altamont all over again. So I snuck another glance and saw Rock mouth to me, "I can't talk to you. I'm with Eddie." I understood. That Rock was a chickenshit. I'm kidding. I was never mad at Rock because he was always half kidding, but I was freaking out enough that Brad noticed. He asked what was going on, so I filled him in with the short version. "I'll protect you," he said. Like I'm a chick. Which I am. Sort of. So I laughed quietly and hoped he was serious.

Whenever I'd see Rock after that, for years, he'd say "Saw Eddie last week. He still hates you." It sort of impressed me that it still bugged him. In a recent *Rolling Stone* cover story, Eddie Murphy was asked about this infamous incident. I was told he said he was mad at everyone about this, not just me. He was mad that Lorne would let that joke through to air. He was mad that the show turned on him, and that's why he has never hosted after that or done the reunion shows. (After that article came out he briefly appeared at the fortieth.) He says he's over this now. I hope that's true.

About a month after that cover story, I was crossing the street in Beverly Hills and I saw a Mercedes Gullwing (a supernice car) parked in front of Coffee Bean. A black guy walked out with a hot blond chick on his arm and got in the car. Like the jerk I am I thought, I wonder who that guy plays for? Then as he started to pull out of the parking lot and I got to the other side of the street, I realized it was Ed Murphy. My old-school fear came crashing back. Should I say something? We hadn't spoken in almost twenty years at this point. Before I knew it, Murphy had spotted me through the windshield. Maybe he thought I was Miley Cyrus. Either way, for some reason I gave a half wave and quick nod. It was my equivalent of the white flag. This can be a risky move if it goes unreciprocated. Then I heard the sound of a window going down. Once again, I was paralyzed by doubt. Do I look? I looked. He stopped in the middle of the street and I walked over. Through the open passenger window he said, "Hey, Spade, how are you doing?" I reached in and shook his hand. I said, "Hey, Eddie. Glad we're good." "Take it easy," he said, and drove away with a girl young enough to be . . . well, my date. (She was superhot.)

My Watergate with Eddie Murphy was over. My burden was lifted. After all those years, that stupid joke can just be that, a stupid joke. And I can go back to appreciating what a funny motherfucker he is.

CHAPTER FIFTEEN

TOMMY BOY

Tommy Boy is the movie people ask me about the most. I've probably been in twenty-some movies at this point, and like every actor I have my favorites and the ones I knew were clankers. Many actors can tell you the list of their favorite movies off the top of their heads, in order, because of the feedback they get. I hear positive comments about a handful of movies I've done and I don't hear jack shit about the rest. Over the years the top five have varied to some degree . . . but the clankers have never changed. Social media makes it super-obvious which of your movies the fans like. Lately, my top three have been *Tommy Boy, Joe Dirt,* and *Grown Ups.* There's a certain fondness out there as well for *The Emperor's New Groove,* which happens to be the only movie for which I received decent reviews. Of course, I was only a voice in an animated film but I'll take it. I'm still clinging to those positive notices. I also hear nice comments from time to time about *Black Sheep*, *The Benchwarmers*, and *Dickie Roberts*. But *Tommy Boy* is the one that is most loved, from people of all ages and all over the map. Which is nice because of all the things I've done, this movie is the one I am most proud of. I loved being on the television shows, but films are a whole different animal. And with *Tommy Boy*, I'm just amazed that it came together as well as it did. At the time it felt completely thrown together, but that was part of the fun.

I was very lucky to be a part of this movie. I was still on *Saturday Night Live* and by no means killing it, but Chris *was* totally killing it. Lorne Michaels, in his infinite wisdom, liked the way we interacted around the office and had a notion to do something with it. We were always hanging out and ripping on each other. I'd make fun of Chris and he'd laugh, and everything he did made me laugh. Chris was actually much sharper than most people thought. You could throw any joke at him, no matter how dry or far-fetched, and he would get it and start laughing, or better yet add to it and throw it back. A lot of people thought Chris was dumb, but that was just an act that he did to come across as funny, and it always worked. With comedy he was very smart.

So, sometime in 1993 Lorne reached out to Bonnie and Terry Turner, the awesome husband-and-wife writing team who went on to create *That '70s Show* and *Third Rock from the Sun*. Lorne told them, "I have a deal to make movies for Paramount. Why don't you guys write something for David and Chris the way they act around the office? Use that relationship and make some sort of big comedy." So Bonnie and Terry went off and came up with a movie about Chris and me as traveling salesmen driving through Ohio peddling brake pads. They put a rough draft of a script together pretty quickly. At that point, the movie was called *Billy the Third*

(A Midwestern), which I thought was clever. This whole movie was a gift, especially to me because at this point in his career, Farley could probably carry a movie on his own—even though it was still early days for him. But this script was ready to go, with an idea that Paramount liked, and it included me! We just had to have the script ready in time to shoot in the summer, during our time off from the show.

This was great news because I don't think we would ever have been able to sell that movie on a pitch alone. I know that. We backed into the whole thing because of Lorne's deal with Paramount and its then CEO, Sherry Lansing. Sherry approved the movie based on the cast, and thank God for that. If she had just heard the pitch—*a movie about two bozos that drive around selling brake pads in Ohio*—well, that doesn't exactly sound like the next *Star Wars.* So we got lucky in that we skated right past based on our amazing marquee names (Chris's anyway). Next, Chris and I read the script. We agreed it was a bit rough but good. Fred Wolf was brought in to do a rewrite and to nail our voices a little better. Fred, Chris, and I were buddies so this was perfect. He eventually became head writer for *SNL.* Lucky for me he knew my voice and the type of jokes I like to do very well. Everyone was on board and happy. We had one tiny stumbling block, which was that Adam was just about to come out with *Billy Madison.* We all decided that both Adam and Chris being named Billy in their first movies was a bad move. So *Billy the Third* was scrapped. However, it was a lot harder than we thought it would be to come up with a new title. We played with *Rocky Road* for a while, and then *The Big Time,* but nothing seemed right. Finally someone said *Tommy Boy* and it stuck. (Of course, whoever said it didn't say this until the end of shooting.)

Fred worked on the script with feedback from Chris and me. It took longer than it should have because we didn't start shooting until the beginning of August, right before we had to report back to New York for *Saturday Night Live*. This situation ended up becoming a bit prickly. We were shooting in Toronto and the idea was that there would be a little private plane, I think a Lear 55, that would take Farley and me back and forth once the show started. I think we got in two straight weeks of shooting before the back-and-forth grind hit. Our schedule became: Monday, Tuesday—Toronto. Wednesday—Fly back to New York for read-through. Thursday—Toronto. Friday, Saturday—New York. And at 1:30 A.M. Sunday, after the show, the plane would take us back to Toronto to shoot that morning at 7 A.M. Now this scared the Spademan a little, because I am what is commonly known around the schoolyard as a pussy. My neck gives me trouble from my little Extravaganza face plant way back when; I need to eat all the time . . . The list goes fucking on and on. It's what doctors call "high maintenance." I'm good for only one thing and that's throwing away jokes in a movie like *Tommy Boy*. So the plan was, shove some Vicodins in my pocket and a protein bar down my throat, push me out there, and then *say some funny shit, you little clown*. Chris came with his own list of challenges. If memory serves, he was not drinking at this point, was in the middle of a sober stint. This was a recipe for more moodiness than normal with Chris . . . and then, well . . . he liked his food. Well, *loved*. Any food, all the time. He switched his addiction from booze to caffeine to get through this schedule. By the end of the movie, I had lost weight and he had gained weight, so the pounds were still up on the screen; they had just switched over to him.

The first day of shooting was the first time either of us had played lead in a film, and we were trying to prep for the overwhelmingness to come. We never had to memorize lines on *Saturday Night Live*, because they were always changing and would ultimately be on cue cards anyway. Pete Segal, our director on *Tommy Boy*, was a very easygoing, affable guy who loved comedy. He was a good presence to have on the set because he wasn't a screaming asshole . . . which I found out later some directors are. He sometimes didn't 100 percent get our odd sense of humor, but he liked us and told us to be as funny as we could, to riff and make shit up, and that he'd try to make sure it looked good and the story worked.

Day one involved three and a half pages of dialogue between just Chris and me in a diner. During the conversation, I realize that Chris (Tommy) is a good salesman. Simple enough idea, right? Being a comedian, I was used to one shot to get something right. Of course, on *SNL* you do your stuff live, so that is only one take. Neither one of us was prepared for how many takes we would have to do to knock out a three-and-a-half-page scene. It was twelve straight hours of saying the same shit over and over, trying to keep it lively and loose because you never knew which take they were going to use. Pete then did at least fifteen master shots of the two of us. Ten over my shoulder toward Chris, ten medium close-ups, and ten tight close-ups. Then he flipped around and did ten to fifteen from a bunch of different angles. Pete called it coverage; we called it smotherage. Chris and I didn't foresee the burnout that would come with all of this. It was amateur hour for us and the movie thing. We were so naïve.

Here's an example of just how green we were. In the morning Chris started the day with a thermos of cappuccino. He would do a small shot before each take to make sure he "gave it everything." After literally twenty-six shots I said, "You can't do this shit anymore, dude. Pete just told me we're going to be at this all day and we haven't even gotten to your close-up. Save it." Chris would go into his trailer at lunch and crash. Hard. No PAs wanted the task of waking him up because they learned pretty quick that they would get their heads ripped off . . . which of course was hilarious to me . . . except when I was on the other end of it. In fact Chris would get so mad when someone woke him up, in such a predictable fashion, that I couldn't resist the chance to set him up. Midway through the shoot, Sherry Lansing stopped by the set to say hello. She chatted with me at lunch for a minute, and then said she'd like to say hello to Chris before she left. This was a typical set visit, but having the visitor be the head of the studio wasn't so typical. It's usually an executive who stops by, not the big cheese. I should have told Sherry that Chris was sleeping but instead told her, "He's in his trailer. I'll have a PA walk you over there, he'd love to chat!" As she was getting closer to the trailer, everyone started looking around with a worried look, knowing this wasn't going to end well.

Well, Sherry Lansing, the head of Paramount, the one who green-lit our movie and was responsible for paying us, tapped on the door of his trailer. "Chris, are you in there?" Here comes the response we all expected. "I SAID I'M SLEEPING AND DON'T WAKE ME UP YOU FUCKING CUNT!" Sherry didn't even react. She just quietly said, "Chris, it's Sherry Lansing, I just wanted to say hi." Pause. Then a completely different, sweet Chris voice says, "Oh, hey, Sherry, let me just get something on, it'll be one sec."

The very next day, we shot the scene where I come to Tommy Boy's hotel in the morning with coffee to announce that we have just made a sale. I knock on the door and say, "Housekeeping?" in a high-pitched Spanish voice. This was something we added to the script when we shot it because I said that to Chris every day at the hotel where we were staying. We stayed on the same floor at the Four Seasons in Toronto during the whole shoot, and when we had a 5 A.M. pickup, I would go over to Chris's room and knock on the door and say, "Housekeeping?" And he would yell, "No thanks!" And I would keep doing it over and over, saying all the things maids say when they come knocking. "Do you want me check minibar? Do you need towels? You like chocolate?" On and on until he would yell, "GET THE FUCK OUT OF HERE. IT SAYS 'DO NOT DISTURB'! LOOK AT THE FUCKING THING ON THE DOOR!"

And then he'd open the door, see me, and quietly say, "Oh, it's you." I'd say, "Yes, it's me, Chris. It's me *every fucking time*. I can't believe you still fall for this." When we shot the hotel scene we threw this exchange in and made something a little flat funnier with our stupid daily shenanigans.

We also couldn't figure out what Farley should wear when he opened the door in that scene. I was pushing for him to come to the door wrapped in nothing but a blanket, which he would drop when he said his last line. We ended up shooting three versions—one of pajama bottoms, one where he is wearing little tighty whities with polka dots, and one where he is totally naked, just for the gag reel. When we did the one where he was totally naked, everyone busted up laughing. He was being shot from behind, but for some reason he turned around to the camera and started moving his hips so his dick would swing in circles and said, "Sherry, do you like the movie?" or something to that effect. Everyone laughed even harder then, mostly out of fear of getting fired. I recently saw those dailies, and rewatched them just to prove to myself that this really happened. I always wondered if Pete stopped that take from getting to Paramount. The studio folks went through dailies every night to see how the shoot was going and a swinging dick might not have sent a positive message. Who knows. Sherry was so cool, she probably wouldn't have given a shit.

As the shoot dragged on, it got harder and harder to keep our spirits up. Chris and I were great friends, of course, and we were having a fucking blast cracking each other up, but there was little downtime and the moodiness and irritability set in. It was human nature. And being together twenty-four hours a day, seven days a week . . . it got tough. It was so pointless for me to fly back to New

York for read-through on Wednesdays because if I hadn't written anything for myself, I wasn't going to be in the show. And I was too burnt out from memorizing lines and shooting to write anything. So by flying back to read-through, I was getting the shit kicked out of me from exhaustion with a sprinkle of humiliation. Chris always had a lot to do in read-through—writers would put him in every sketch because they knew he was a score machine but he was wiped out, too.

A lot of things come together from different angles when you're doing a comedy. Every joke is so fucking important that you rack your brain all day to try to make things better and better. The best jokes are almost never in the script that was handed in the day before the shoot. I would imagine that in a drama, you don't have that much leeway. (I wouldn't know. Lifetime has never called me.) But with a comedy, especially if you have a good enough team of actors, directors, and producers, you can keep adding to the bitter end to make the movie funnier. I know Judd Apatow, Will Ferrell, Sandler, all the funniest guys out there do this. Even an editor who is on his game can get you so many free laughs. A good editor is so important. Our editor, Bill Kerr, was great at the extra gag. Three days after we shot the scene in a gas station where Farley breaks the doors off, Kerr showed me a rough version. He had done it so that the scene cuts to me being sarcastic to the attendant, and then to the attendant, and then back to me again before we even say another line. Stuff like that is so crucial to the final product. We got three laughs instead of one. He also threw in the song "Crazy" droning in the background. Another nice touch.

One of my script ideas was the scene when Chris and I are driving along after a long day of sales. We are both burned and tired and the really fruity song comes on the radio. I pitched the idea to Fred that the song should be one by the Carpenters. (This comes from my REAL LIFE, because I had *The Best of Carpenters*

CD in my car, and once a girl got in and turned on the radio to find that disc blaring "Rainy Days and Mondays." I played it off like "What is this shit?" and then acted like I didn't know it was even in there. I may have even tried to blame her.) The scene in the movie based on that is pretty funny, especially with the final beat being the hood of the car popping up and we spin out. It is joke to joke to joke. Fred was good at placing ideas like that, then adding to them.

One other bit that we threw in at the last minute was the scene right before I whack off to the girl at the pool. It was sort of flat and jokeless until I see her out the window, so I asked if we could weave in a bit I had written for Weekend Update a few weeks before. (I was still trying, in my lame way, to get on the show.) The bit involved me reviewing movies, something along the lines of: "You know which comedian liked this movie?" (And there'd be a picture of Cameron Diaz.) "Buddy Whack-it." "You know what baseball team loves Cameron? The Yankees." "Who was your favorite Little Rascal? Was it Spanky?" And on and on. All those jokes were loaded in to that update bit (which bombed at read-through, by the way) but I had such confidence that there was something funny about it I asked if we could put it in and dish those payoff lines to Chris because it made the most sense. It was not a big scene but it made the existing one a bit funnier with him nailing those. Also, when Chris walked by the hot girl at the pool and said, "Is there a weight room?" or whatever, all those takes were classic Farley making shit up and killing. Props can also help a scene, too. I love that exchange when Chris tells me he's wearing a clip-on and I go, "Are you sure?" Throwaway jokes like that are important. They don't get huge laughs but they're nice texture and they carry the style of your humor across. And often they pass by so quickly it doesn't matter if not everyone laughs. Those are my favorite kinds of jokes, the ones that pay off the tenth time you see the film.

As I write this I feel like I sound like I'm patting myself on my back, claiming that I wrote every joke in that movie. I didn't, of course. I would just add in my ideas here and there and try to hold up my end of the deal. This movie was obviously a tour de force for Chris and made him a movie star. He was hilarious in it. Bonnie, Terry, and Fred wrote a great script and Fred added jokes the whole way. Chris added in his own killer stuff. The one thing I did a lot of was rely on my memory. I could remember all the funny shit Chris had said in the past. I would tell him to say them when I thought they would work on-screen. And Chris would say, "Davey, that's a great joke, thanks." And I'd say, "It's your joke, dude; you said it a year ago."

We finished the movie and Paramount seemed pretty happy with the test screenings. When it was released, it was number one for the weekend. That shocked a lot of people, including us. Neither one of us had much of a concept of whether we had fans, or if anyone even gave a fuck about us at all. So to see the movie debut so strong was a nice boost. Today, all these years later, it's still talked about, which I guess means it has stood the test of time whereas many of my other on-screen performances (or gems, as I like to call them) have not. I have to say I definitely got spoiled with *Tommy Boy* because I didn't quite realize how fucking hard it is to get a movie to number one, to get it to be pretty solid all the way through and memorable ten years later. People forget that making a shitty movie is just as hard as making a good one. That one was sort of lightning in a bottle.

After *Tommy Boy* worked, Chris and I went on to shoot *Black Sheep*. The story behind *Black Sheep* is complicated, and there are a few different versions out there. I'm going to tell you my version, how I remember it. Sometimes people remember things differently, but this is my recollection. Paramount wanted another movie with us after *Tommy Boy*. The timing needed to be that we would write the movie during the *SNL* season, and then shoot during our summer break again. It was interesting working backward from a green light. I don't think there was ever another time in my career when I experienced this, and I can say now that this was a luxury. But the problem was that after *Tommy Boy* was considered a success, everything got way more complicated. That movie was Chris, Fred, and me making up shit and having fun, with no one on our asses. For this movie we were being watched like a hawk and the clock was ticking.

Fred Wolf wrote up a quick first version of a script and handed it in for Chris, me, and Paramount to read. This was where things got tough. In a strange turn of events, I was going to make more money than Chris on this movie. The reason was that Chris had been in and out of rehab, and had made a two-picture deal with Lorne and Paramount. I'm sure he signed it to get back in everyone's good graces, to show he was a team player. He had a set fee for the second movie. My fee for *Tommy Boy* was a one-shot deal so I got to negotiate from scratch for the follow-up. So that was awkward, but we got past it. The real elephant in the room was that Chris had quietly been offered the lead in *The Cable Guy* for $3 million. This was an unbelievable amount of money and nothing close to what either of us was going to make on *Black Sheep*.

I came to work one day and Chris was there, hair all greased back, smoking a cigarette, and in all-biz mode. He said, "Hey, have you read *Black Sheep* yet?" I said, "No, I'm reading it tonight. How is it?" He said, "It's good, not great. I think it needs a lot of work. There are some good moments but we should really take our time with this and get it right. Probably wait until next summer." I left and went to an Au Bon Pain café underneath Rockefeller Center. I went there to think about the situation. It was very unnerving. I knew that if I didn't like the script and said no to doing *Black Sheep* that summer, Chris would be off the hook with Paramount and could do *The Cable Guy*. But if I liked the script and said yes, Chris would have to do it because he owed Paramount a movie. So I had to take his script comments with a grain of salt because maybe he was telling me in between the lines to just say no to this so he could go do *The Cable Guy*. I decided I would read it with an open mind and just go with my gut. If I didn't like it, I wouldn't do it, and Chris could do whatever he wanted. That night I read it and realized it wasn't perfect but there was a funny movie there. I thought we could work with Fred, pepper in our extra jokes, and everything would work out fine. This had a chance to be as good as *Tommy Boy*, in my opinion. So I said yes. This didn't go over great. I told Chris, "I'm sorry but if you took *Cable Guy* out of the equation, you know this movie can be really good."

Chris came around, but it was an uncomfortable moment. Luckily, he faced reality and decided to focus on making a great film.

Now for the next problem we didn't see coming. To direct the film, Paramount hired Penelope Spheeris. She was a hot director coming off the success of her documentary *The Decline of Western Civilization* and then *Wayne's World*. Of course, that movie was a massive success and starred two *SNL* comedy leads, so it all sounded perfect to everyone but Chris and me. Trouble started right away. Penelope told us right off the bat that she didn't love *Tommy Boy* and that she knew how to make Chris and me funny. That's where someone should have pulled the plug. Then she ripped forty pages out of our script and said she would fix them with her writer. Fred and she had a few bad meetings and he was essentially kicked off the project from then on. She was making so much more money than us, she outranked us and that was hard for Chris and me to deal with. I wish Pete Segal would have done it but he was tied up. We all had it down and could have really made that thing a crusher. My gut told me Mike and Dana had made all the comedy decisions on *Wayne's World* but for some reason they were giving the credit to Penelope. I didn't get it.

In the movie, Chris and I shot a lot of scenes apart. This was odd, because the whole point was our chemistry. We were always funnier together. Chris was also asked to make the relationship between him and his brother slightly more dramatic, which I didn't mind, but I personally thought the movie should be straight comedy with as many jokes as we could cram in. I could tell she really thought Chris was a great talent. Unfortunately I could also tell she thought I was not. It was package deal, and unfortunately for her I was part of the package so she had to deal with me. The shoot went all right but we had troubles along the way; it was just not a good match. Once there was a scene where I ran around singing "Summer Lovin'" from *Grease*. The idea was that I would be out in the woods, singing at the top of my lungs, when I am caught by a bunch of tough hunters. Then I would immediately switch gears and talk about how I wish I was blowing the heads off antelopes with my trusty twelve-gauge, never acknowledging that I had just been prancing around singing "Summer Lovin'"—both the Danny and Sandy parts. Twenty years ago this probably would have worked but it was not funny to Penelope. At all. She kept telling me she didn't like that scene and wanted it out. Fred, Chris, and I stood our ground. We wanted to shoot it, but promised to get rid of it if it didn't test well. Seemed fair.

The day of that shoot (another scene Chris wasn't in) we were twenty miles outside L.A., in the middle of nowhere. We set up a crane shot and I was waiting in my trailer. I was all by myself . . . waiting . . . and waiting . . . until finally Penelope knocked on my trailer. She came in and shook her head. "I can't do it. I'm not shooting it. I can't put this scene in my movie. I hate it." There was a pause while I went over my options in my head. I finally said, "Okay, got it. That's a wrap." And we all went home. With no cell phone, no landline, and no way to get to Lorne . . . there was nothing I could do, so I had to eat that one. Penelope has said since then that I have never made her laugh. That made a lot of sense to me. She just couldn't say it out loud back then. I know my comedy isn't for everyone but in my opinion, she never should have taken the job.

Despite all of that nonsense, the movie came out and still did pretty well. I liked a lot of it and so did Chris. We by no means hated it. There are fans who still really like that one and even a few who like it better than *Tommy Boy*. But if all the jokes and scenes that we came up with had been included, what that movie could have been when Chris was at the height of his popularity and on top of his game . . . that movie could have been fucking unbelievable.

A FEW MORE THINGS ABOUT CHRIS

As you can tell if you are reading this book, Chris Farley was a big part of my life, for a small amount of time. After what happened I got to chat with Danny Aykroyd about what happened with John Belushi. It was nice to have a cool dude I looked up to let me open up and ask questions on how to handle it all. I will always be remembered by many people first and foremost for the things I did with Chris. I'm all right with it.

Chris and I were so young and stupid on *SNL* and when we made our movies together. We thought we had it all nailed. I think we can all agree that he did. I was still learning, and happy to be his straight guy, hanging on for dear life in the tornado that was Farley. But more than the comedy, it was the fact that Chris was my friend that was the important thing. Our bullshit at *SNL* carried me through the times when I wasn't exactly tearing it up on-screen, or in the writers' room. I could rely on him to make me laugh or to laugh at my jokes when no one else would.

I wanted to share one more story that perfectly represents the nature of our personalities and our friendship. Not many know this story aaaand I wish it was classier but . . .

Once during our *SNL* stint I had the amazing luck to be dating a *Playboy* centerfold. Being the tool that I am, I had to puff up and bring the *Playboy* to work, bragging to my friends that I was hooking up with this hot chick. I showed the pics to Chris, Adam, and Chris Rock, and after a few high-fives and fist bumps (so street) we went to the read-through. Well, during the read-through, Farls sends me a crumpled note (no cell phones then) that said, "Did you look in our office yet?" I looked at him confused and he smiled like a psycho Cheshire Cat and then nodded and giggled. I was like "whatever." Then on an intermission he asked again. I said, "No. What the fuck is in the office?" He just laughed and said, "You should look." Then laughed a sinister laugh he usually did in the Gap Girls sketch. So I walked to my office with the others in tow only to find the *Playboy* magazine open on my desk, and the centerfold was covered in jizz. Chris's jizz.

Yes folks, you heard right. He hustled out a jack-off sesh right before stressful read-through and was so proud of his work. He was behind me when I walked in and saw it, as were Sandler and Rock. We were all a little shocked, even though we thought it was funny. And gross. And crazy. Chris looked around at all of us, taking in our reactions. I could tell by the look on his face that he was suddenly worried he had gone too far. That made it even funnier. Chris *had* gone too far. He did every time. That's what made him Chris. And the fact that I was such a lame little shit that I had to bring the mag to work to brag to my buddies, like a teenager, I deserved a hazing. I'm not sure that was exactly the hazing I would have guessed but it was a great example of how "out of the box" he thought. This was borderline psycho.

Chris always went right to the edge, and often over it. Taking things too far is the thing that made him Chris but it was also the thing that took him away in the end. I miss the guy every day.

CHAPTER SIXTEEN

SKIPPY

Hiring an assistant is a very difficult thing for people like me. Being an assistant to a celebrity (cue eye roll) is a vague job that everyone thinks is easy because you seemingly need low to zero skills. And zero schooling. Most people think it's a total cakewalk. One of the first questions I get from model/actress types when they realize things aren't going perfectly as planned in L.A. and that they may need some steady income (and don't want to be hookers yet) is, "Hey, do you know anybody that needs an assistant?" They are like, "What do I do? Just pick up dry cleaning, gas up cars, fly to New York on a private jet and hang backstage at Letterman, hit premieres, and fuck off the rest of the time? Sure, I can handle that." This was the type of assistant I had, when I first hired one. So I guess there's a reason they think that. My first assistant was an old friend so she just hung out and shot the shit with me and did what she wanted, when she wanted, because I'm a softie, I never yell, and I am easy to work with. Naturally, they take advantage of me. I'd tell her to come over at 10 A.M. and she'd roll in at 10:45 with a Starbucks going "The fucking 405 was nuts today!" I would sit there thinking, *Well, this isn't new information. No one ever says, "If you want to save time, take the 405. Best-kept secret in L.A. Shhhh."* The 405 is nuts every day! Then she said something to the effect of, "I can usually make it here in twenty if there's no traffic." Well, when's that? Christmas Eve? Any other time it's fucked. Never say "if there's no traffic." In L.A. that is not a real scenario.

When that one left to have a baby, I had to hire a new assistant. This time around I interviewed a guy and a girl. I knew the guy already. He was named Skippy. Well, that was his nickname. His real name was David but since I had dibs on David we went with Skippy to keep confusion down to a min. While I was deciding between Skippy and the chick, I got the unforgettable call that Chris Farley had been found dead. Since Skippy had worked for the director of *Tommy Boy* (that's how we met), he knew Chris and knew me and knew all the parties who would be involved dealing with this disaster. So I just hired him on the spot.

By the way, I should say here that Skippy is six foot two and about three hundred pounds. He was a very nice guy, laughed a lot, was funny and easy to be around. Once on the set of *Tommy Boy*, he had been caught at the wrong place at the wrong time and I felt bad for him. Chris and I were doing a scene where we had to wait outside a house before going in to see Rob Lowe and Bo Derek. Unbeknownst to me, Chris was pissed at me that morning. The night before when we landed in Toronto, Chris had said he was sick and going to bed. I called Rob and asked him if he wanted to get a beer. And I found out later Chris didn't like that. Why? Because I was sort of his wife. I mean, we were so close that it was weird. He was jealous that I called Rob and didn't tell him. Now, I'd seen this angry look from him before. He would kind of bite his lip and stare at me. And it sucked, because it meant storm's a-brewin'. It was like looking at a grizzly. I could run or try to make myself bigger.

I should have known that something was up because while we were sitting next to each other in makeup, Chris kept mumbling, "Where's Rob Lowe? Hmm? Where's Rob Lowe?" I just said, "I think he's on the set." And he'd start again, like Travis Bickle or some shit. Everyone's eyes are darting around thinking "Um what's going on?" So a few minutes later we were, outside the scene and waiting for our cue to enter. It was freezing. I was sitting on the ground eating a tuna sandwich and he was staring at me. Grinding his jaw, biting his lip. And staring. Eventually I said, "Can I help you, sir?" (to be a smart-ass, if anyone can picture that) and he stepped on my hand and sandwich, which were both on the ground. I popped up (this is the making myself bigger part) and threw my Diet Coke on him (so *Basketball Wives*). Then he pushed me down five stairs. And this was the textbook beginning of a street fight. Not a UFC fight, or actually any fight in history, but we were about to go at it. And by go at it I mean I'm about to lose quickly to this Ronda Rousey mothafucka. "ANNNND ACTION, DAVID AND CHRIS!" we heard over the walkie-talkie. We stared at each other for a beat then casually walked into the scene. I had the first line. I just stared, silent because too much was going through my head. Pete the director yelled, "What's David's line!?" The script supervisor said it. I walked off set. Pete was like, "Ummm, okay, let's take a five."

So I went to my trailer and Chris went to his, like Mariah Carey and Nicki Minaj. We were two divas arguing about God knows what. Fred Wolf went to Chris and said, "You can't go after Spade like that. We have a movie to finish. I know you guys are tired. And he's smaller than you. If you're going to fight, you can't go after a dude that weighs 130." This pissed Chris off even more, because Fred was not taking his side (not that anyone even knew why we were fighting). Chris calmly got up and looked out the window of his trailer to see Skippy walking by. He bolted out of the trailer, ran over, and tackled Skippy hard for no reason other than that he was pissed at me. Then he kind of laughed, and walked away. Skippy was dumbfounded but you can't talk back to number one on the call sheet so he sort of chuckled and limped away.

Skippy was my assistant for about three years. He did a fine job. We got along. He did some improv comedy on the side. It was all good. Having an assistant means that you now have someone who helps do all the kinds of shit work you used to do when you were struggling. When you have an assistant it's such an odd thing because all my life I was doing these kind of jobs. Valet parker, dishwasher, busboy, clothing store assistant, etc. So now to have someone working for me was so weird. I still wanted to be the "cool" boss because I had had so many dicks in the past. (Let's not take those last eight words out of context.) But eventually, some weird shit started to happen. All was normal for a long time. But then I saw some odd things, like NBC asked if I wanted Dodger tickets. I told Skippy to say no . . . mostly because if you take something from the network, then down the line they can come asking for a favor in return.

And sure enough, I got asked for a favor down the line. I said no. They say, "Hey, come on, we gave you all those Dodger tickets." I went to ask Skippy. He said, "They told me I could use them if I wanted." Okay, so I'm still thinking, *Don't be a dick about it. It's an honest mistake.* Next odd thing is when I heard from Rebecca Romijn and Kid Rock (name drop!) that my assistant had texted them. Just to say what's up. Nothing business related. Hmmmm. But the one that really hit me wrong was when he asked for a part in *Joe Dirt.* (Applause. "Oh, a few of you remember that one? Thank you . . .") I told him I would see what was possible but that I didn't have final say. Skippy was big, funny, and likable so I figured that maybe he could do it. But when we were almost ready to film the movie, Adam Sandler called me to suggest Kevin Nealon for the part because Adam thought he'd be funny for it. I agreed. Kevin's always solid and Adam's my boss. Easy enough.

Now is where things got weird. I broke this news to Skippy and he was disappointed, but then that quickly turned to pissed. "Tell Adam it's already taken, tell him no way." I said, "Skippy, I get that it sucks but there's no way I'm telling Adam no, on the one thing he asked for. He's the reason this movie is getting made. He never asks for anything. He likes you and has no idea I held that part for you. I'll keep my eye out for something else." I should have paid more attention to this little exchange with Skippy, because that's not how an employee should talk to their boss, even if their boss is a cool guy like me.

Cut to a few months later. I was sitting with Skip while editing *Joe Dirt*. He saw the scene with Nealon and said, "There's the scene Adam fucked me on. I would have nailed it." That attitude took me back. I told him Adam didn't fuck him and to let it go. Then we ate dinner, and he went on his way like usual.

At about 5 A.M. that night, I had a gross feeling that someone was watching me while I slept. I looked up to see a shadowy figure standing in the doorway to my bedroom, wearing a baseball hat and with his arm behind his back. Needless to say, I was scared shitless.

It was Skippy.

I was out of it and weirded out. I mumbled, "What are you doing?" "Um, the alarm company called, it went off." He then looked over in my bed to see if anyone was there. Then he said, "So there's no one here, you're all alone?" I started to stand up and said, "Yeah, sorry they called you. I don't think I even turned it on . . ." and WHAM!!! He hit me in the face. I fell back. He punched me a few more times as I fell back on the bed. I then rolled across the bed quickly and popped to my feet on the other side. When I looked down I saw blood on the bed. I didn't know what the hell was going on. I said, "Skippy, what the fuck are you doing?" It hadn't sunk in yet that I was in a brawl and my nose and back were bleeding. He just stared at me blankly, like a robot on a mission. He had a stun gun in the hand he'd been holding behind his back, and was hitting me with it along with his other fist.

I ran to the back door of my room, which opened to the yard, but I didn't have enough time to unlock it, so he grabbed me and threw me to the ground. (Dude is big.) I stood up and my vintage *Coneheads* sleeveless T-shirt came off in his hands. (Funny movie, *Coneheads* . . . well, parts were funny.) For a sec, we just stared at each other in disbelief. I scrammed knowing I still had a chance to escape, running out the garage door, into the driveway and toward the front gate. Of course my high-class celebrity security means that my gate needs a code to open, even to get out, so I'm in the Hotel California—I can never leave. Plus, I had no idea where I would go even if I could have gotten the gate open. It was 5 A.M. Who was going to open their door to a crazy guy screaming? Plus Skippy was on my ass like a cheetah. So I jumped behind one of my old cars. Skip was on other side. I was starting to get tired, but also realizing that this shit was for real. Picture getting up to pee in the middle of the night and how out of it you are . . . this dreamy state was how out of it I was and then I'm getting the shit kicked out of me. It was not a dream. And it sucked.

I see him staring, crouched with his stun gun and ready to fight. I say fuck it. With the last bit of energy I have, I run right at him. I hit him and we go to the ground. By some miracle, I get into a position where I can punch him, and I start whaling on his head with both fists. As I'm doing it I realize that it fucking hurts. (I suddenly felt bad for UFC guys. Hitting a head is like punching a rock.) *And* I was hitting my friend. One punch landed perfectly and he dropped the stun gun. I squirreled away and then hauled ass into the house, slamming the door and trying to flip the dead bolt. WHAM!! He hit the door. This fucker was unstoppable. I fell on my back and gave up. I accepted my death. BUT, thank God, the dead bolt had closed just enough to keep him out. I took my chance. I ran to my bedroom and slid under my bed, where I keep my loaded shotgun. The only other person who knew it was there was . . . you guessed it . . . Skippy! (The police later told me that his plan had been to incapacitate me with the stun gun, go get my shotgun from under the bed, and kill us both. Fun theory!) I went into the bathroom and locked the door. What the hell was I going to do? I looked in the mirror and there I was with my pajama bottoms on, no shirt, bloody face, scratched arms and back. (So I think, This would be a great Instagram picture. No, it was ten years too early, unfortch.) The pad of my big toe had caught on something and was flopping around, bleeding. I was feeling weak and could feel the adrenaline dissipating (good word).

I realized that I needed to go call the cops, because if I passed out in my bathroom at 5 A.M. no one would find me. Then it occurred to me that I was going to have to shoot my friend. (Great friend, right?) I was not happy about this idea. I screamed out, "HEY I'M COMING OUT AND SHOOTING YOUR LEG FIRST, THEN I'M SHOOTING YOU IN THE FACE. I'D GET THE FUCK OUT OF HERE." I paused, then I kicked the door open. He was gone, thank God, because I would have hated to shoot someone. I peeped around the room . . . no Skip. I hobbled to the phone and called 911 and for some stupid reason, I didn't rat him out. I told them that some six-two, three-hundred-pound guy came into my house and beat the shit out of me and to get over here. And that I'd be waiting in the alley behind my house. I went into the alley with my shotgun, wandering around with blood on me. Eventually the cops show up and motion for me to lay the gun down. One says, "You're okay now, we have guys inside searching your house." I was coherent enough to say, "Well, you don't have to look *everywhere* . . . he's not in the drawers . . ." (I said this know-ing I had some shit stashed around my house, heh heh.) Lo and behold, old Skip got away. The news vans were already pulling up to my house, in another nightmare plot twist.

I was glad to be alive. I didn't want to blab to the media (though I probably should have and milked it). The cops pulled Marc, my manager, aside and asked him why I was covering for someone. It was clear to them that I knew my attacker, as they say in cop-speak. I think I covered for Skip because he had been a close friend, for a long time. I also knew that he would be toast if I ratted him out—it would be jail for years. But when the detectives told my manager they thought it was a gay sex thing gone wrong, I sang like a canary.

They found Skippy later that day parked on the street, very woozy and out of it. In his trunk they found rope and duct tape. That was unsettling at best. They said he had taken 125 Tylenol PMs. (Maybe he wasn't trying to kill himself, but when I take a half of one of those, I'm out for ten hours.) Skippy went into the hospital, and I went into a hotel for a few days to chill the fuck out. The cops said I could press charges. I never did. I asked them to get him psychiatric help so I could find out what the fuck actually happened. In my mind drugs alone don't make you turn on a buddy like that. I couldn't make sense of it. This guy wasn't a criminal mastermind. He just flipped out. Or just hated me, I'll never know.

He also had a clean record and I was a bit worried he would get out of jail in six months and pull a Max Cady from *Cape Fear* and come finish me off. So I tapped out and moved on. But ulti-mately I did have to move to a new house, because even after the blood came off the doors and the carpet I was always scared to sleep in the old one. Even my therapist said I was being a pussy but I couldn't help it. So I moved and got a new assistant. A girl. Who weighs 110 pounds. So I could for sure take her if shit went down. Well, 90 percent sure.

CHAPTER SEVENTEEN

MY FIRST HOOKER

was with a hooker once. It was a mistake. I mean it wasn't a mistake to sleep with her; I don't care about that. It's that I just did not know she was a hooker. (I can feel you rolling your eyes. But it's true.)

I was in Las Vegas (the first sign that something bad is about to happen) and I was walking past a day club where there was a line to get in. A very normal-looking cute girl asked me for a photo. (Side note: When someone asks me for a picture, I almost always say yes. Ninety-nine percent of the people who ask are very cool. The only drawbacks are nervous sweaty people, because shaking hands with them is like shaking hands with a ShamWow, and the people who are hot and put their arms around you. They press their stinking sizzling pit into my shoulder and it basically brands me. Especially at the pool in Vegas. Hot stinky pit branding on my bare

shoulder is so gross. All I can think of is sssssssss Sizzzlerrrrrrr . . .)
So I took a few pictures with this girl, and then she invited me
into the club, which was actually inviting me to stand in line with
her. That seemed like a drag. Maybe she wanted me to skip her
to the front of the line. Either way, I let her off easy, telling her I
had to get home. She hit me with the digits (new term for phone
number—super new) and told me to give her a call the next time I
was in Vegas.

Two weeks later I just so happened to be back in Las Vegas. At
the time I had a deal with one of the hotels on the Strip to perform
twelve weekends a year. I had done the Mirage for a few years,
and then Planet Hollywood, and also the Venetian. I loved all of
these spots and had great gigs there. I won't say which hotel this
incident occurred in, because if word leaked out that a hooker was
seen in a hotel in Vegas, all hell would break loose. Vegas would
shut down tomorrow. I don't want that.

Being the gentleman I am, I texted the young lady whom I had
met in the club line to see if she remembered me and wanted to
meet for a drink or perhaps come for my shitty show. She quickly
answered back, "What are you doing right now?" Hmmm. This
seemed a bit unorthodox because most of my courting happens at
night and this was the middle of the day. Daytime is odd. Stiff.
I don't day drink so there's not much to say or do, especially in
Vegas, unless she wanted to take a romantic stroll down to Glitter
Gulch or Slots of Fun, but I didn't even know her. I replied, "I'm
golfing with some idiots." In fairness, all of my friends are all idiots. I need new friends. Anyway, she answered back, "What about
before the show?" Ummmm?? I said, "Well, I usually get ready in
the room?" That was the most basic/uncreative answer possible. I
had no clue where this odd exchange was going. "Maybe I'll just
come by the room," she texted back.

Ooo, now I knew where things were going.

I was stoked! Clearly this chick was into me. Maybe she wanted a hot beef injection before the show. (Hi, Mom!) Could it be this easy? I mean I would usually take this more seriously but she's setting the casual tone. She was slutty and I didn't see a big future with her so I saw no problem. If she wanted to rally, I was all for it.

So I finished my golf game and headed back to the hotel.

Knock knock . . . and there she was at my door. Now I was nervous. I had zero booze in me. I was noticeably weirded out because I had no idea what to do next. Do I make a move right away? Maybe she just wanted to be buddies, or talk about *Joe Dirt* or have me leave a funny message on her friend's voice mail (I get that one more than you might think). But no. She sauntered in and looked out the window.

"Nice view," she said, not really caring.

"Oh, that old fifty-mile, gorgeous view?" I joked, weakly. She barely registered that I had spoken and she started to strip, folding her clothes into a neat little pile. Next she took off her rings. I thought, *Oh shit, it's about to go down! Places, everyone!* When the rings come off, you know there will be some dick grabbing happening. Then, she dropped the bomb . . .

"So it's eight hundred. Up front."

Immediately, I freaked out that she was a cop. I didn't know what to do, but I sort of wanted to go through with it anyway, because I didn't want to look like a pussy, and I wanted to get laid. (Hi, Grandma!) You know what I mean, guys. Who's with me??!

My mind is swirling. What if I hand her the money and she slaps the cuffs on me? What if it is a trick and she takes the dough and then goes and blabs to the tabs? Please don't be a tab blabber! Listen, my dick doesn't shoot up north in record time on a normal night, if you get my drift, so this confusion didn't help. But finally we got down to action Jackson. We start to go at it and to be honest, girls don't like it when I fuck them anyway but this girl really couldn't stand it because it was all biz. And of course she makes me wear this rubber she gives me that's made of Gore-Tex or something that hookers make in a hooker supply factory, so I had literally zero feeling in said dick. It's not good when both parties say, "Is it in?" at the same time. "Jinx! Hahahahahahahaha!"

But seriously, I can tell she's just going through the motions . . . "Oh babe, so hot." Like a robot (hooker robot). Missionary, doggie, back to missionary. Then she says, "Cum for me, babe." Which translates to "Let's wrap this up, old man, I have to be at the Bellagio in twenty."

Then, to top off this nightmare this call girl actually *takes a call* during boning, which is . . . I don't know where that falls in the book of etiquette, but my boner left the building, so to speak. And that was that. Dear Abby would have a field day with her behavior.

So that's my hooker story. She wasn't a cop but now there's another chick out there who thinks I don't fuck good. Great.

CHAPTER EIGHTEEN

MY HOUSEKEEPER

Another situation you find yourself in when you get a little cash is you have to hire a housekeeper. This makes a lot of sense, because most people hate doing chores (me) and don't have time with all this fancy famous-people work shit to do laundry and dust off the Emmys (that I may get one day). Laundry is something I truly hate. I hated it in college and I hated it when I did stand-up on the road. The act of going to a grimy local Laundromat somewhere in Tulsa with forty-five bucks in quarters in a pillowcase and sitting there staring at a dryer sounds fun, but it isn't. I hated laundry when I was on *Saturday Night Live*, because I had to spend my one day off, Sunday, going down to the 100-degree cavernlike basement in my apartment building and check on it every ten minutes because people would either steal your shit or put your wet clothes on the folding table if you waited too long. Whatever it is, it is all bad. Plus, because of the *SNL* hours, I never had any time during the week to go to the bank for my quarter addiction, on some weeks I was super hosed. So long story longer, I now have a maid. You know, a housekeeper . . . She's a maid, though, come on. I don't know what to call her. I'm a grown-up now and I live by myself but I can't pull my shit together so this lady helps me.

My housekeeper always had two people with her whenever she came to work. This is usually the drill in the wilds of Beverly Hills. This particular maid had a daughter and another woman with a gold tooth who tagged along. A gold FRONT tooth, mind you. That's pretty hard to hide, but I guess what's the point of a gold front tooth if it's hidden, right? Maybe I'm overthinking. She was like the Lil Wayne of maids, I guess. This girl with the gold tooth was pretty cocky in my opinion. She was always shining her tooth with her T-shirt on company time. Which was gross (and sexy). Actually not sexy. It's 100 percent gross. I get it—you were rich one day of your life and bought a tooth instead of a car. Fine. Quit subtly bragging. An odd reality of housekeepers out here in Los Angeles is that they always seem to bring a floater/helper. And you can never keep track of who's who in your house. I think it's meant to confuse you. It's a lot of razzle-dazzle to keep you off balance, and it works. I don't like strangers in my pad to begin with, and the maids bring in a plus one for "extra help" once in a while or when they are out "sick" and send over a replacement or a fill-in they met at IHOP. I don't know. It is all unsettling. I don't know who is in my house and who is on the clock and on my dime. I'm always like, "Where's the main maid who I sort of know??"

But the main maid was smart because she was orchestrating this shell game. She got more time off and I stopped asking who's who. Genius move. One time, she actually had a good reason to skip two weeks of work. She said, "David, I'm going to be gone next Friday for three weeks, but the strangers will be here working so you are covered." I was a little taken aback, because two to three weeks seemed like a long time. "Why gone so long?" I asked. "I'm having my baby," she said. LIKE I HAD ANY IDEA SHE WAS PREGNANT! (I'm so self-centered I didn't notice.)

I felt so dumb. I said, "Um, oh . . . right . . . cool . . . ya, no problem. Take your time. I'm sure . . . uh . . ."

"My daughter and Gina can handle it." She knew I didn't know anyone's names.

"Sure, ya, they are good." (I figured Gold Tooth must be Gina.)

Obviously I have a ton of embarrassing things around for a maid to see. This is the hard part. My maid knows me back and forth. She sees girls stop by, she sees famous people coming and going, and she knows when I'm acting like I'm working in my office but probably whacking off. She sees empty booze bottles, a renegade Vicodin in a pants pocket here and there . . . etc. . . . etc. This chick is a Google search on my life. There are no secrets. And since she's been with me for years, she's really got the 411 on old Spadeyboy. This makes me nervous, and especially now because what she knows she may have shared. One of those details is that I always have a fair amount of cash in my house. I get money delivered (baller alert) and I keep it in an envelope because I don't go to ATM machines. (I gave up on them years ago. I don't want to get shot. I think everyone's getting shot who uses them. And I know they have cameras at ATMs that are supposed to keep you safe, but that just means there is a video for TMZ after the fact of me getting shot with a handful of twenties. Not super comforting.) So I get a bunch of tens and twenties and some c-notes (rapper talk) brought home and I keep them in an envelope in a drawer in my dining room. Over the next few months, I was plucking them out as needed and it seemed like a bit was missing. It isn't enough to make me freak out, but I felt confused because I thought I had more dough stashed away. Then, one day, boom. A lot of it was gone. I didn't know what to do. I got scared. Maybe the maids were pinching? Maybe I was being careless, tipping too much like Scrooge McDuck or making it rain a lot, who the F knows? But I didn't go to the cops yet, because I'm a moron.

Then it was Christmastime, the time of year when I yank out a lot of cash to share with my family and friends because Christmas is the time of milking (me). I decided to get smart, so I put the cash in a duffel bag, which I partially zipped. Only partially, because I think, No one can get in this. It's foolproof. Who's smart enough to think of unzipping it?!? Three days later, it's almost Miller time. I hit up my bag and IT'S GONE. ALL OF IT!! WHAT THE HAY IS HAPPENING?! I stare at the bag. Nothing. My first thought was that I had thrown the money away. Honestly. I did not immediately think that I'd be robbed. Especially by my housekeepers. There was a lot of money in that bag and I was always around. It would have taken *Ocean's Eleven* to plan this caper. It would have been too ballsy and in my face. So I went to the main maid, who was then back from her maternity leave, and asked her if she'd seen the dough in the garbage. (I realize it is a dumb question. Me: "Hey, did you see a bunch of money in the garbage?" Main maid: "Yes, why? Did you not mean to throw it away?") She has no idea what I am talking about. I don't know what to do. Something's wrong and I think it's me. This is like when my parents got divorced when I was four and I thought it was my fault. (Later I was informed it was.) I'm just a mix of confused/pissed/weirded out.

So I went to the Golden Globes to clear my head as one does, and who do I see but the lovely Kate Beckinsale. She's a doll. She was there and she's all like, "Blah blah blah . . . How ya been . . . blah blah blah . . . You're so funny . . . blah blah blah . . . You're a genius . . . blah blah blah . . . I wish I was single." You know, small talk. We were there talking, and I don't remember the exact convo but then it popped into my head that we have the same maid! Can you believe it? So I immediately asked, "How's the laziest maid in America?" (Just to be hilarious.) And she said, "Lame! In fact I'm missing ten-thousand-dollar earrings. And some other shit!" HOLY FUCK! All the puzzle pieces are suddenly fitting! I've cracked the case! I don't know if I was more excited about this or about the fact that I had been seen talking to Ms. Kathrin Beckinsale. I shook off my joy of discovery and said, "Oh my gosh! I'm missing over ten grand in cash!" (Sorry I sound like an asshole but that's not a lot when you see bigger assholes on Instagram flaunting way more. You heard me, Floyd Mayweather.) And she said, "I think it's Gold Tooth." And I agreed: "Yes, yes! Fucking Gold Tooth! She's shady as shit. Always shining up her grille. It has to be her . . . So what do we do?" Kate has no ideas. "I'll think of something." Then Kate drifted off into the night and I stood there, soaking in my new info (and some Belvedere).

The next day I called my business manager. He's like an accountant but does more and costs *wayyy* more. I caught him up with the sitch and told him to fire all the maids. (I don't want to do it because I'm a pussy and she might rat me out to the Cartel for being a snitch.) "You can't just fire someone," he said. "Even if they are clearly ripping me off?" "Nope. They can sue you." Wait, sue *me*?? What's happening in this world? No one can get fired anymore. I seemed to have no problem getting fired from every job I had back before I started doing comedy. Then he piped in with this brilliant idea: "We will get a private investigator to figure this out." "Oh no, no, no, I don't want a sting operation going down in my house. I'm too freaked out." But I finally agreed because it seemed like the only way I might see my Benjamins (rapper term) again. So now "Operation: Where's my fucking cash" was in full effect. Two days later these two scary dudes come over and break down the whole plan for me. It was like a plot from a *Fast and Furious* movie. I just sat there and nodded my head, like Vin Diesel does. I actually didn't understand what they were planning at all, but I played along. Next the guys took out a camera pen and filmed my duffel bag for about thirty seconds. "This will be used later," he told me. Thirty seconds didn't feel long enough to me. I didn't even know if they were real private eyes but they looked like Ray Liotta so I went with it.

The next day the maids were supposed to arrive at nine thirty. The private eyes came at nine and walk me through the Big Sting. My first clue that something was amiss should have been when I saw the ladies roll up in a new Land Cruiser with twenty-two-inch spinners, but all I could think at the time was, "How was the Kendrick Lamar after-party?" But once they got out of their fat ride the idea was that the detectives would split up the maids and grill them separately in different rooms. Divide and conquer. Each was going to be asked the same series of questions, with the hope that one would be caught in a lie, get scared, or narc the other one out. The lead undercover detective was fluent in Spanish, so he let them have a quick chat before separating them to catch any last-minute cover-up plans.

I wanted to bail on the scene because I was cringing at the thought of seeing the maids all confused and upset. And if they weren't guilty, I would feel like the biggest asshole in the world. All those people on Twitter will be right! So I got out of the house pronto, and ran over to a breakfast spot and sat monitoring the phone, texting Kate B. updates (along with some dick pics; until her husband sent back bigger dick pics). After I had my usual breakfast of Diet Coke (I know, gross) I got the first text from my assistant: "They took them into different rooms, it was scary!" Of course I had made her stay and watch them stare at her with the same look dogs give you when the vet takes them back to have their nuts chopped off. That betrayal look. It's brutal. Ten minutes later I texted, "What's happening?" She said, "I don't know I'm hiding in your office!" "No, no, get out there, get on the front lines, I want to hear all the deets!" Eventually she texted me back. "Ok big news, Gold Tooth cracked! She admitted to taking $500." And I said, "Holy fuckarolli, have them roll up those sleeves and keep going with the waterboarding." An hour later she admitted to ten thousand dollars! This chick was singing like a canary! Now you couldn't shut her up. Meanwhile the main maid wasn't saying shit. She was the Whitey Bulger of the gang. Hard-core. No squealing. I wish I had been there. I would have told them, "I don't care if you steal a few Planet Hollywood jackets from me, I mean, just keep it to a minimum. I get it. I have some money, my life looks easy. I know you're going to steal from me, that's not a problem. Just don't go nuts and make me look like an idiot. I mean ten grand?!" So we let them drive home and the guys met me for postgrilling orders. I didn't have them arrested. But they are down to working only two days a week (lololol). The best part was that Gold Tooth told the detective it was all my fault for leaving the money lying around. She pulled the old dipsy doodle.

So, remember when they filmed my bag for thirty seconds? That turned out to be the clincher. In the interrogation room, they set up three phony monitors. Then they put the thirty seconds of footage of my bag playing on one of them, and had my assistant guide the maid into the room so that she could see it when she walked in. The detective yelled out, "No, no, no we're not ready yet, get her out of here!" and they turned it off real fast. Of course, the maid knew the gig was up then, and thought that she'd been filmed picking Benjamins. She started singing right away. She admitted that for years, every time she came over she would take at least two hundred-dollar bills. EVERY TIME. Do the math. That's a lot of money. Shocker of the centch.

The next whammy was that I still couldn't fire the main maid. She hadn't yet confessed. I needed to force her to confess, and somehow we did. She wrote it all down and said it on camera. I sent a copy to Kate B. as a birthday present.

So the lessons I learned were . . . don't be rich. And try to be a better hider of money. And buy a pen camera. And don't have a gold tooth.

Maybe I got the wrong lesson from all of this.

CHAPTER NINETEEN

A VICTORIA'S SECRET PARTY

Twitter and Instagram are pretty new to the world (compared to the wheel), but I'm finally getting used to them. I skipped MySpace for the most part and even skipped Facebook initially because I never believed they would catch on. That shows you how smart I am. But in my defense, MySpace, if you recall, was mostly about music in the beginning, a place to hear someone's lame band or bad raps. MySpace sort of replaced demos. I always hated people handing me demos, especially my friends, because once they hand you their music demo it's a ticking clock until they ask you to give them feedback. And rarely can you make this feedback honest. No one really wants to hear negative stuff about their "tracks" and they'll usually just grumble, "What the fuck do you know about music anyway." They have their response covered whether you like it or not, so any feedback is pretty pointless. Another problem is when my two rocker buddies used to catch me off guard in my car with their dogshit CD. That was always horrible, because before I could say no, it would be, "Hey, I just so happen to have a copy of my band's latest crummy tunes right here. Let's pop it in. By the way, the mix isn't final and vocal mikes were fucked that day but you'll get a feel for it." Really? This is your sell?

And besides that, what if, in some miraculous chain of events, I decide to give your shitty disk to Guy Oseary or Kid Rock or any other important legit music guy who could sign you? This is the pitch I get? This is your best swing? I'm supposed to picture a song I don't really like 20 percent better? Not possible, you dumb fuck. No contestant on *The Voice* says, "Hey gang, before I start just FYI, I'm super-hungover and my voice sounds like Lindsay Lohan's after a guy from Dubai just jizzed a sand load down her throat but let's try this." So I'm always stuck in demo jail in my car. I can't leave and I can't roll down my window. I just have to stare and fake-listen to noisy squelches that will never see the inside of an iTunes store. And I don't even know where to look; do I stare at the actual CD player? (yes) or do I act like I'm into it by slightly bobbing my head (sometimes) or God forbid do I look over at my musician friend air drumming or singing along with such intensity that I know it's an act because he's heard this song five hundred times already and can't be this into it? (I try not to. So embarrassing.) Usually I just quietly count to three minutes in my head and hope it's over then so I can say "cool" and sprint out of my car into traffic.

But my point was, I didn't get tangled up in MySpace for that reason, but when Facebook popped up I thought, Oh fuck, this isn't going away. Now there's another version of this dumbness. So I waited a year hoping this small fire would burn itself out but *noooooooooo*, it got bigger! So I finally joined. I gave in. So after getting caught flirting by not realizing how it works I pared down the people I follow. I can't believe a guy invented this because it's such a great tool for women to bust guys cheating! Girls know every nuance of how Facebook works, that's what I have learned. It's a never-ending bust. I don't even know half the time why I'm getting caught because girls will never explain how they figure it out. And by the way, these are just girls I'm casually dating. God forbid I was married or had a live-in girlfriend. I don't know how my friends do it.

I finally jumped in with Twitter about a year after it started, and I got on Instagram even faster because I realize the fans get mad if you don't engage a bit. Plus, I ended up liking engaging with my fans. The movie and television studios now actually look at how many followers you have to help decide if they want you for a part (true story). They want actors to use their "socials" to help them get the word out for free on their projects. All of this is actually a great deal for the money people. You blast out shit to two million people and it's like a little commercial on a low-rated show. But it's still a lot of reach. Twitter started out big, but Instagram passed it fast—at least with my friends. I think Twitter is now mostly writing jokes or saying clever things about your life and some people just have trouble with that. And I get it because doing that is fucking hard. Unless you're writing, "I had Funyuns today," then it's tough going. I try to be clever and within 140 characters it's hard to do and I'm supposed to be good at this. I know some ladies who get a brain cramp because they all aren't Jerry Seinfelds and don't have a keen eye for observational comedy, which plays so well on Twitter.

Instagram, on the other hand, is perfect for the gals. When the chicks of the world heard there was a new invention where all you do is take pictures of yourself, your food, and your dog, fist bumps all around. Holy shit this is too good to be true! A lot of them left Twitter in the dust and focused solely on the business of Instagram. (Snapchat is even easier! Instead of a picture of your cat, it's a twenty-second video of it!) This is all causing problems for me. Instagram gets me *really* nailed. My problem is that it's so easy to track your whereabouts with all of this shit. It's like LoJack (old reference). YOU CAN'T LIE ANYMORE, FOLKS!! DO YOU GET IT?! THIS IS A PROBLEM! Honestly (hee-hee), lying is a thing of the past. If I tell someone I'm busy for a night and can't hang out, they can just type my name into Twitter and suddenly it's forty Spade sightings all over the place. You can literally track a person's night like connect the dots. "@DavidSpade is on my flight to Arizona!" (Photo of back of my head.) Then "just got a pic with Joe Dirt @DavidSpade at Hertz counter in Scottsdale." Then "@DavidSpade is next to me on freeway with some chick. I think he went to school here #ASU." So you can see how this is a problem. The girl I blew off will call me and say, "How was your night?" and I'll be like, "Oh, pretty chill, just laid low." "Really? Laid low in fucking Arizona? My friend saw you there with some brunette!" (By the way, it took me four years to realize that her "friend" was the Twitter time line.) "You're an asshole!"

Instagram is the same shit.

GIRL: Who's this chick Stacey?

ME: Stacey who?

GIRL: Some whore. You liked her picture on Instagram. Are you fucking her?

ME: What? No. I don't even know her.

GIRL: So you stalk some girl and like her pictures but don't know her? What a creep.

ME: No. I mean I kind of know her, but how did you even know?

GIRL: My friend told me! (Also known as staying in for six hours scanning Instagram like Tom Cruise in *Minority Report*. Charts and graphs all over.)

ME: (Bummed-out expression on face.)

Once, an ex met me in Newport for a night. I told her no pictures, no posting, no bullshit. (That should be a sign in every establishment, replacing "No shirt, No shoes, No Service.") I didn't want to get caught by the chick I was currently dating. (Great guy.) Then I saw that she posted a pic of herself lying out by the pool. The shot was a close-up, so you couldn't tell where she was. Well, that was enough to set off the bloodhounds. My new girl followed the ex, or at least ghosted her (hip social media lingo). So if I was at a place that has sun, and the ex was also there, that was all the new girl needed. She went into *Murder, She Wrote* detective mode and got her answers.

GIRL: So how is golf in Newport with your buddies?

ME: (Getting nervous because this is a weird question.) Um, good.

GIRL: So you're having a good time, just you and your guy friends?

ME: (More nervous, WTF is going on?) Ummm yeah, yeah, all good in the hood.

GIRL: So it's just you and no chicks. Just guys weekend, like you said right? And don't lie. I'm giving you a chance not to lie.

This is the worst thing chicks do. I never know if I should bite on this hook because I have to quickly guess the odds of how much the chick already knows. I rarely come clean in this situation, mostly because I'd always rather put off a fight than have it right then.

> ME: Umm . . . sticking to my story, babe. Just dudes,
>   yawn . . . actually pretty boring.
> GIRL: You're such a fucking liar. (Hangs up.)

I was confused. I started accusing my friends of ratting me out because this girl always texted them just to say "hi" and she'd use her evil genius to trick them into giving up vital and bustable info.

> Example: GIRL: Hey Steve, I know David still hangs out
>   with that girl Amy. It's cool, we talked about it. I just
>   want to know is she nice or a bitch?
> STEVE: Um, she's pretty cool I guess.
> GIRL: Oh that's good. (She never knew I was still talking
>   to Amy, but now she does!)

It's a chick trick (more on those later) and she loved to start this kind of civil war. And my buddies are so fucking stupid they fall for it every time. I'm always overly concerned with how I'm found out. The chick would always tell me it didn't matter how she knew, but that I needed to address the charge levied against me. I would plead that if the accusation was based on emails obtained from my laptop, that was inadmissible evidence. Girls don't play by the same rules as the court system. Unfortch.

Anyway, this brings me to the only Twitter story worth a shit that I can share. Through the magic of the social media, I got to meet one of the most beautiful girls in the world. Here's what happened. One day I was walking around in Beverly Hills with my crooked stupid trucker hat on trying to look cool as per usual, and I stumbled upon a Victoria's Secret store. In the window was a huge photo of Candice Swanepoel, a sickeningly hot import from South Africa who puts 99 percent of girls to shame. In the photo she was modeling the latest underpants or whatever, and I thought, Ooh-la-la, let's take a picture of this to share with all my horny guy followers. Great idea right, but what's the joke? I couldn't just post a pic for guys to beat off to, and at least half of my followers are female, so if I make it sort of clever at least they'll laugh (maybe).

So I held up a penny in front of Candice's poster and took a picture of it. My brilliant caption was "Oh look at this sexy, hot penny." The penny was tiny in the foreground and then behind was this whole picture of her. Now it looked kind of amusing, but it wasn't some home run of a joke. But that was fine. It was a broken-bat single. They can't all be gems. I figured it was funny enough to throw out there to the Twitter gods. I fed them one more day, my work as a comic today was done. Well, luckily this one happened to get a lot of play. I got some favorites and a lot of retweets. (So gross that I noticed.) Now, when this happens there's a chance you'll get burned by some Twitter rats. Twitter rats are the losers who rat you out to other people when you do jokes about them. Like they'll say, "Hey @KimKardashian did you hear what @DavidSpade said about you?" They want to get you going in a Twitter war, which I would rather avoid. (Isn't it sad that we live in a country where Kylie Jenner can't drink or vote but she can be in a Twitter war?) I never put the "@" with the celeb name when I do one of those kinds of jokes, because I just want to get a burn in and be on my merry way. Plus, the Twitter rats will likely take care of it for me.

Well, Candice found out. Now, in all fairness I've laid down some harsh jokes on Twitter, but calling a girl beautiful isn't the worst one. And Candice wrote on her Twitter that she thought the joke was funny. Well la de frickin' da! This babe knows I'm on the planet! This was great news! I was shocked by this. I didn't plan to do anything about it. But my idiot friend said, "Dude. Send her a DM. Just say hello." I thought this was a bit nuts. I mean, first I needed to make sure that the page was actually legit. It panned out so I decided to embarrass myself and send a direct tweet. For those of you who don't know what that is (my grandparents), it's like an email. If you both follow each other then the lines are open once a direct tweet happens, and you can send messages no one else can see. So I rolled the dice. I said something like, "Hey glad you were cool with that joke. Keep up the good work," or something similarly weak and gameless. I left it at that and went about my day. Well lo and behold the next day there was a notification that I had a direct message from her. My friend was shitting. I played it cool and waited about eight seconds before I clicked on it. She wrote, "Hey there. I laughed. It was funny." And in my head I'm like, *Boiiiing oooinnng ooinggg* (that's a boner noise) and in my pants I was like *Boiiiing oooinnng ooinggg* and then, like a dumb fuck, I wrote back. Immediately. I didn't wait a day like you're supposed to, I didn't even wait ten minutes, and I immediately started pecking away. Again, gameless. To make matters worse, I said something like, "That's great maybe I'll run into you someday." So lame, especially when you consider that her message really didn't require an answer at all. It was a statement, not a question. But that didn't stop me. No sirree.

But later that night, there it was: another message from Candy. "Hey are you going to go to the Victoria's Secret party in L.A. next week? If so, come say hello." And I go, trying to be cool, "Oh, I might swing by." Meanwhile it's another round of *booooiiiinggggg*.

I told (bragged to) my friends, who were all stoked and wanted to tag along. Luckily, my buddy Cade works with Victoria's Secret and had sent me an invite so I had a legit reason to go. The day of the event, she messaged me again. "So, are you definitely coming tonight?" And I was like, "RELAX babe, don't be so thirsty. Fucking Needy Gonzalez. Take it easy. I might pop in." I didn't really write that, but we were all laughing at how redick we were all being about this party. My buddies and I cruised in, got a juicy booth, some booze. I see Candy Cane. Now I was nervous. "There she is," my idiot friend said. "Are you going to go talk to her? You going to talk about Twitter?" And I go, "No, that's stupid, dude. We'll talk about other stuff." So I slugged down a few shots of Belvedere and primped my fluffy feathered nineties hair and sauntered over. I was getting closer and she was getting prettier. Cade made the introductions. "Candice, this is David Spade." I say, "Hey, how are you doing?" You know, I was playing it all cool. "Hi" she said. And that was it. "Hey," I said. And then silence. Again. "Having fun at the party?" "Yeah." Finally I couldn't take it. "Hey, on Twitter, thanks for liking that joke about you. I know it's stupid but that was nice, you were a good sport." And then, as if in slow motion, she looked at me funny and said, "Oh no, I'm not on Twitter."

Wuhhhhhhhhhhhh????

I looked at her like a dog watching a magic trick. It wasn't quite sinking in. I couldn't hear anything. I stood there like an idiot just staring in disbelief. Finally she jumped in with "Oh, was there like some fake account that says it's me or something?" I was dying of embarrassment. I didn't see this coming at all. To add insult to injury, she said, "Oh, what was the joke? I'm sure it was funny." It was like when a bomb goes off in the movies and there is that high-pitched noise over total silence. I grabbed my ears and staggered away in slow motion.

I walked back over to my buddies, who were all desperate to hear what happened. I couldn't even talk. And then Miranda Kerr, another lovely, sweet Victoria's Secret model, came over to ask how I'm doing. I managed to mumble something like "Uh, ah . . ." and she asked why I was crying. (Kidding.) So, I just told Miranda the whole story. She couldn't have been nicer about it. She even felt bad for me. And while I was coming out of this Candice jet wash I slowly realized that the other hottest woman on the planet was actually supercool and supersweet and was A REAL PERSON, not a fake Twitter account. Eventually, we all had a laugh at what a fucking dipshit I am.

I still can't believe I got catfished, though. It can happen to anyone, guys. I was so fucking stoked to meet Candice and she had no idea who I was. She probably thought she was meeting a contest winner or something. Serves me right for trying to beat the internet.

CHAPTER TWENTY
CHICK TRICKS

This chapter is a lot shorter than you might be expecting, mostly because I'm not married and my love life is sort of a disaster, so any relationship advice I give should really go in one ear and out the other. I have a reputation for dating tons of girls. This probably started back in the *Just Shoot Me!* days. Finch, my character, was hitting on models in every scene. Most of my rep comes from the characters I play on television and movies, and generally my characters chase young women. I'm not even sure I can play anything else, to be honest. I've never been asked. Now Spade the real guy isn't exactly Finch or Higgins or any other number of skirt chasers I've played. Obviously these characters are exaggerations—I try not to be so desperate and obvious when talking to girls in real life like, but that doesn't mean I am good at it. And even though I'm not good at it, that doesn't mean I don't try.

I'm an average-looking dude. It is different for me than for someone like say, George Clooney, who is far from average. This guy had been single all his life, up until very recently. People have tons to say about my being single, saying things like "The guy's fifty. I mean come on, it's just not cute anymore. When is he going to get his shit together? I always see him with a different girl, it's so embarrassing. Act your age and get married already . . ." But with someone like Jeter or DiCaprio, the hens on *The View* and those other shows say things like, "Why should he get married? He's single and loving it! Let those guys have their fun. They're rich bachelors; having the time of their lives . . ."

I always wondered why Clooney caught a break on that and I didn't. I think it's the good-looking factor. At least that's what I'm blaming it on. I heard a quote once that has been attributed to Clooney but I'm not sure he said it. Supposedly when someone asked him, "Why aren't you married? Aren't you afraid of being lonely?" he replied, "The loneliest I've ever been was when I was married." It's a great quote whether GC said it or not, and probably hits home with a lot of married men and women out there. Some people have marriage wired. I'm not totally against the trip down the aisle, but I don't think I've found a situation where I could nail it perfectly. I've dated great girls. Especially in the last few years so it's more my problem. I'm not anti-marriage, I'm anti-bad-marriage. But now Clooney has caved in and gotten married and I'm sure will have a kid by the time this book comes out. That surprised me. Plus he was the one guy I could point to as a cohort in the bachelor game when people were busting on me. By the way, I have nothing against Clooney; the guy has always been cool to me. He even showed up at the *Black Sheep* premiere and took a picture with my mom and danced with her so he's okay in my book, married or not.

I also heard a great tidbit about Derek Jeter. (Do you like how I put myself in the same company as the best-looking/most famous actor and the best-looking/most famous athlete? . . . I do.) Word is that after he hooks up with a chick, he sends them tickets to a Yan-

kees game or a signed uniform. Genius. So ballsy. Again, I don't
know if this is true but I have incorporated it into my life anyway. When girls leave my house, they can take either a *Joe Dirt* key
chain or an *Emperor's New Groove* throw pillow. If they're still not
happy, I tell them there's a box of irregular Kate Spade purses in
the garage . . . grab one on the way out . . . limit one per customer.

So now that my preamble has gone on too long, I wanted to
share some wise words for you dudes out there. Take this as you
will, as it is coming from a guy whose longest relationship was three
lap dances in a row. I call them Chick Tricks and a few Dick Tricks.

Dick Trick: Try to stop telling your date you think every other
girl on the planet is hot. You'd think this would be a no-brainer, but
for some reason, I did it forever and I'm not sure why. I've finally
stopped. Remember, girls are smarter than us, and find sneaky
ways to prove it all the time. One method is to tell you that every
guy you ask about *isn't* hot. They have this down perfectly. Whenever I'm with some beautiful girl and she's looking in a magazine
and I say, "Would you fuck Brad Pitt? He's hot, right?" they're like,
"Yuck. No. Not my type." And then I'm happy. Two days later, I
say "Oooh, Johnny Depp is in a new movie. I bet you'd fuck him in
like two seconds." And she's like, "No way, he's gross. He's so old
and such a weirdo. He looks dirty." I'm like, "Really?" (And believe
it.) Then she pulls the switcheroo. "What do you think about Jes-
sica Alba?" Of course, I say, "Oh my God, she's so fucking pretty!"
She's like, "Oh really? What about Rosie Huntington?" I say, "Holy
shit, she's a fucking ten." "Would you like to have sex with them?"
Like a dumbass, I say, "Of course! . . . all day, every day! Why, is
it possible?!" She just stares and it finally dawns on me that I have
said something wrong. She's got that look like I was supposed to
know that she was only ACTING like she wouldn't fuck Brad Pitt
and Johnny Depp. "Don't you get what I'm doing? OF COURSE

I WOULD, YOU MORON. THESE GUYS ARE BEAUTI-
FUL. I'D FUCK THEM ON THE HOOD OF YOUR CAR
IF I COULD. PLAY THE GAME, DIPSHIT!" And then I
realize . . . I probably shouldn't have given my real opinion. I will
not fall for that again . . . until she asks me about Jennifer Law-
rence or any waitress . . . (By the way, I'm bluffing when I say I'd
fuck anyone "all day, every day." That's a lie. More likely it would
be twice a week; once Monday and once Thursday or Friday, and
both of those would be about six minutes of boning combined with
a lot of wheezing and talking about myself in between . . .)

Chick Trick: If you're a promotional model and you're forty,
it's time for a new vocation. Handing out Miller Lite key chains
in a bar during March Madness is a four-week gig, not a lifelong
modeling career. At twenty-two or twenty-six, it's not a bad time
killer to earn a few bucks, but when you're still dragging out the bi-
kini to hit the bar and talk to a group of guys you would have done
anything to avoid ten years ago, it is time for a rethink.

Dick Trick: If you're with a girl and you want to bring a sex
toy into the relationship, buy it new and have her watch you take it
out of the package. One time a girl asked if I had any toys, and I
pulled one out of a drawer. She said, "I don't think I'll be using the
community vibrator." This made me laugh, partially because it was
so accurate. Not cool, guys! Think!

Dick Trick: When you meet a girl and start dating, they often
say, "I'm not into games. Text me whenever you want, let's just
keep it real." Girls who say they don't want to play games are playing the best game of all. This phrase makes you drop your guard so
you're not on your game, and that way they read you a lot easier and

can get more intel. It's a trick that gives the chick the upper hand, and when that happens that early it's just a ticking clock before she dumps you.

Dick Trick: If you're texting a girl after midnight, the fewer words, the better, because there's absolutely no reason to text her unless you want a late-night booty call. Keep it simple. If her phone is buzzing, she knows what you mean. I usually go with something simple like, "Yo yo yo." Simple, elegant, and to the point. Or the more direct "Where you at yo?" My angle is to talk like a rapper; it helps give me much-needed "edge" and "street cred." Sometimes I add "where's the po-po?" Girls love this. You can also try "You home homie?" (Inject humor, then inject ween.)

Chick Trick: Ladies, relax with your birthday hype. I'm done with the whole "birthday week" thing. That is one thing I cannot stand. Don't you get enough attention? After the age of nine, birthdays should naturally taper off on the excitement meter. But girls have a weird way of making birthdays a bigger and bigger deal as time goes on. Let me tell you a secret, ladies. Everyone hates your birthday week. Guys hate it because they don't know what the fuck to do on your actual birthday, let alone on the real estate before and after that you're also marking off to celebrate yourself. And other girls really hate it because the focus is on you consistently for seven days. Don't you realize it's hard enough for them to focus on you when you're in a conversation with them when all they're doing is waiting to talk about themselves again? And to be so self-centered that you expect these other selfish bitches to have laser focus on just you for a whole week, is really redonkulous. And if you're ever wearing a tiara during this so-called birthday week, you need to get clocked in the head with a baseball bat by your mom. It's em-

barrassing enough you're barking out orders of where your brunch
is going to be and what to wear to the pool party, and the don't-
forget-to-bring-me-a-present-every-day bullshit, and the pouty
look you give your best friend when you realize she is wearing the
same outfit on Monday that she did on Friday. Hey, she's not going
to shop for your birthday week and come out in different dresses
for breakfast, lunch, and dinner like Carrie Underwood hosting
the country music awards . . . FUCK YOU NO ONE CARES. Be
more realistic. On your actual birthday night, try to get six bitches
to sushi on time and not fight over the check for thirty minutes.
Make them all pay for you and keep the tiara in your purse and
you may keep your friends for an extra few months. *Birthday Week*
should be a movie starring Kristen Wiig, not an actual thing you
are desperately trying to organize for your life.

Chick Trick: Ladies, I think it is funny how sometimes you
program a guy's number into your phone with a description instead
of a name. That way, when a dude calls, you don't have to think
"Who's Jeff?" You can just look down and see "Douchebag, from
Boa" or "Poss Gay Bartender" or "Stamos-Lite" or "doesn't wear
condoms." Guys do this, too, but it's for craftier reasons. It's usually in case his girlfriend sees his phone. Instead of Nicole, it might
ring as "Joe's Plumbing" or something else possibly work related to
fool the wife. But when "Chico's Lawn Service" calls eight times at
2 A.M., they know what's up.

Dick Trick: I have two bathrooms in my master bedroom. It's
a house from the 1970s and during that time, they often built his-
and-hers bathrooms, which is actually a blessing. The problem is I
don't use the hers very often, only women do. One time, an Aus-
tralian girl I was dating accused me of cheating. She apparently

brought her tricks across the ocean with her because she finally got me to confess. I found out later she knew I cheated because she took a photo of the inside of the shower and the way the shampoos and soaps were lined up when she was there. The next time she came around, they were out of place. She went ballistic. I don't want CSI Melbourne on my case twenty-four hours a day so we had an amicable (horrible) split-up. Guys, if you have a chick bathroom, don't keep any soap or shampoo in there at all. Make them bring their own and take it with them.

Chick Trick: If you're casually dating a guy, you can find out pretty easily if he's married or has a girlfriend, other than you, around special occasions and holidays. Thanksgiving and Christmas really show his cards . . . birthdays, too . . . but the biggest bust of all is Valentine's Day. I've heard girls say, "We're going to go out the night before Valentine's Day because he's working late on the fourteenth." Or, "It's such a zoo at the restaurants he doesn't want to deal with it so he's going to take me out next weekend." *Girls—these guys are married!* Or at the very least have a serious girlfriend. Don't be the February 13th or 15th girl. Push hard for the 14th or you're officially the designated side action.

Chick Trick: Don't tell a guy his dick is small, no matter what. Even if you both know it is. If you're watching a porno with a guy, never say, "I don't even like guys with big dicks," because it immediately sounds like you think the guy you are talking to has a small dick. I've had girls really hammer it home to me, and then catch themselves. They start by saying, "Your dick is fine." When they say "fine" I already know I want to tap out of this conversation. *Fine* is like the word *okay;* it's a shoulder shrugger . . . it's a C on a report card and no one gets excited about a C on a report card. (Unless you're Nick Swardson.) This same girl just started blabbering and couldn't stop: "I hate big dicks . . . they hurt . . . it's sore down there for a week . . . I keep thinking about it all the time . . . it makes me scream a lot during sex . . . I tell all my friends about it . . . it never fits all the way in, it's a hassle . . . I like yours. It doesn't hurt, at all . . . there's zero pain . . . my mind drifts off during sex . . . I try to figure out my week in my head . . . I never think about it after . . . it never crosses my mind . . . it goes all the way in easily, it's perfect." I say, "Oh that's great, good for you." I'm disappointed and know it's a burn, but to guys sex is like doing laps in a pool—if you can go in there and touch the end and come back, we're good, right? How much fucking extra do you need?

Chick Trick: When you see a guy's cock for the first time, any guy, I don't care if it's your uncle, make sure to make a big deal out of it. Make the guy feel good. When the pants come off, gaze upon the cock as if it is a diamond, nestled in black velvet at Zales jewelers. Pepper in some oohs and aahs to spice it up, add to the excitement. Say things like, "Oh my God!" or "Holy shit!" Get creative: "That thing is NOT going in me." (I've never heard that.) Or, "Let me just stare at it for a while." Or, "I wish we could make a dildo out of this, it's so amazing." Do not do what happens to me 97 percent of the time, which is that I whip it out with sort of a "ta-da" attitude and the chick just stares at it without making any expression at all. She might mumble in a slightly disappointed voice, "Okay, let's do this." The worst is when you can tell they really are let down, because they add, "You know what, why don't you throw it in my ass while you're at it. I always wanted to try it and this will be like a practice run in case I really do it someday. I just want to get a feel for it . . . YOLO, right?" And I say, "Yeah, cool. YOLO, I guess." That one stings.

Chick Trick: Don't audition plans when a guy calls to ask you out. It's bad enough when my guy friends do this to me. Me: "Want to hang out tonight?" Friend: "Why? What's going on?" Me: "I don't know, maybe eat some tacos, chill." Friend: "Nah, I think I'm going to stay in." Me: "Sorry, it's not courtside to the Clippers game, you fucking asshole, then you'd be available, right?" Friend: "Exactly." With girls it's worse because they take it one step further, checking out the plan to see how Instagrammable it is. This is a new thing and it is very real. Me: "Hey, do you want to come with me to a gig in Albuquerque?" In their head, they're thinking, "Flight on Southwest . . . no good pictures there/too embarrassing to post while sitting in coach . . . Then we will be in the lobby of the Holiday Inn Express hotel . . . no good snapshots there . . . Backstage at the Giggle Barn Comedy Club . . . me next to a plate of four Triscuits and a Slim Jim? . . . that's weak." She says, "No thanks, I'll pass on that date." Me: "Oh really? Well next week do you want to see the Rolling Stones in Hawaii? We're taking a private jet." For this one it is all "Pic of my feet up, me holding a piña colada . . . I like that . . . Photo out the window of the islands & hashtag it #almost there . . . good . . . Photo with Mick Jagger . . . 'Look who ruined my selfie! Lol . . .' #blessed." "Yeah, that sounds good, I'll go."

Dick Trick: When trying to get girls to watch porno, try to sell it like a real movie to hook them in. "Babe, this is just like *Pirates of the Caribbean*. Except no pirates. Aaaand no Johnny Depp. No story and just a bunch of random fucking." You're not Roger Ebert, relax and give it a chance . . . stop being Penelope Prude.

Dick Trick: The more girls trash their exes, the more they are in love with them. It took me forever to figure this out. If you're hearing six months later what a dick this ex is, run, FAST.

Dick Trick: Avoid the girls who talk too much. I think they do this to seemingly bond with a guy they like. They love for you to call them to chat. I hate when they ask, "Can you call me?" Or, "Can you call me right now?" Or, "Can you call me when you get in the car?" Or, "Can you call me when you get up?" Never date these battery burners. Any chick who keeps you on the phone twenty minutes a day is a drag. I always try to stick to texting, because there is less chance of triggering a blab-alanche with that mode of communication. Never ask, "How was your day?" because that's just pulling her string. You'll never get another word in once that thirty-minute run-on sentence starts. Sometimes I will just say to a girl, "I gotta get off the phone, it's almost nine." And they say, "Nine P.M.?" And I go, "No, nine percent battery. I started with one hundred. I'm hanging up."

Dick Trick: Don't call a young girl on the phone when you first meet. This sets off her "old man" radar. And my God, never, *ever* leave a voice mail. I once heard two twenty-four-year-old girls talking about a guy one of them had met. She thought he was cute, but she decided she wasn't into him. When the other asked why she said, "Oh my God, it's so embarrassing, *he called me.*" And the other girl goes, "Oh no, gross. What a loser." I had to chime in, "Wait, is that bad?" And of course, that immediately set off a loser alert on me. "Of course. I gave him my number to *text* me. What the fuck am I supposed to say to this guy if he calls? You walked by me last night at the club that was fun. Tell me your life story." The other one then pipes in with, "Holy shit, speaking of losers, I had a guy leave me a voice mail last week." So I'm sitting there darting my eyes knowing I've made this blunder and ask, "Well, what did he say?" She says, "Who the fuck knows? I didn't listen to it. Are you kidding me? Who would leave a voice mail? I don't even know how to listen to them." I was in shock. This is so odd because I'm from the days where girls get mad if you *don't* call, so this is all new to me.

Dick Trick: When you meet a girl, there's some clear signs you can pick up early to know if she actually wants to hook up or if you're going to be a buddy. The first sign is if she calls you "buddy" in a text. "What's up, buddy?" You're dead in the water. Another one is being referred to as "silly." You text her, "Where you at, yo? Why don't you come by?" And she answers, "I'm at home, silly." No girl is planning on fucking you if she calls you silly because that's a name they usually reserve for an eight-year-old nephew. Also be very careful of lunches. I hit on a girl for a year when I realized I had settled for three lunches in twelve months. It was time to hang up the cleats on that one, it's not happening.

And, for my final words of wisdom . . .

Dick Trick: Never tickle a girl when she has diarrhea. Take my word for it, the fun stops quickly.

EPILOGUE: THE TIME I DID TOO MUCH COKE

I miss coke. You know, cocaine? Or whatever we used to call it. Coke, toot, blow, rails, lines, blast, chalk, powdered Pepsi, devil's dandruff, sniffy jiffy, power flour, booger sugar. It was all the same to me. Great. I got introduced to coke the first year of college. One of my fraternity brothers was a part-time dealer to help pay for school. I guess that counted as a work study job? It definitely beat working in the cafeteria.

Let me back up a bit. I had decided to go to Arizona State University, and was pledging SAE. I had a job, too, working part-time in a men's clothing store. And I was trying to do stand-up whenever I could. All of this added up to mean that I was always tired and always on the verge of flunking out of school. I used to be the chess and spelling bee champ, and now I was a dumb-ass. This was a very hard adjustment to make, to be honest. So there I was, flopping around school all out of it when one day my entrepreneurial frat brother said, "Do you need a bump?" These were magic words I would learn to fall in love with.

He explained that "a bump" was just a small amount of cola on the back of a pen cap. (Thanks, school supplies!) It was nothing to be afraid of, and I just had to sniff it. So I took a toot and WOOHOO! SOLD! I loved it! The coke woke me up, I felt great, I was in a good mood, and there was no downside whatsoever. So now I'm skipping around campus, doing my shitty pledge chores and telling someone a thirty-minute story! It was a perfect day!

Well, my buddy had created a monster. From then on I was constantly knocking on his door like a little junkie trying to get a snootful: "Just to get me through my econ class." He caught on pretty quick that I was hitting him up too often for the freebies, and since I wasn't a hot model he was trying to sleep with, the well dried up quick.

"Twenty-five bucks," he said through the door.

"Come on man! Just let me smell it!" (I was so clever. Heh heh.)

Professional dealers have little to no sense of humor. He was all biz now. "The smallest amount I can sell you is a quarter gram, which is twenty-five bucks. But this is really good shit." I realized later that every single dealer says their shit is good shit. The truth is, it rarely is. This guy was literally the only guy I can recall who actually had really good shit. It took ten years for me to realize a lot of dealers sell terrible shit, mixed with Lidocaine, Fruit-Fresh, baby laxative, or soap. It's always a drag to do a line and immediately say, "Do you have a bathroom?? I have sudden UNCONTROL-LABLE DIARRHEA! IS THAT SEXY, LADIES?!" Anyway, I coughed up the twenty-five dollars out of my student loan and got my very first amber vial, one-fourth of the way full of cocaine. Red-letter day.

Unfortunately, I was not good at rationing my stash. It went a bit too fast. Now that I didn't have to ask for the drugs, I used my own judgment. My own judgment apparently was a bit off because the next day I needed more. I had chipped away at it during class, at my valet parking job. (I needed the cash. Now for coke, apparently.) Then at the club before going onstage then after. I even did some the next morning during breakfast. Who needs coffee! I've got blow! But once I was down to zero, I realized that I needed to carve out some of the budget for this. My student loans and part-time gig checks were spoken for with tuition, rent, and food. There was no such thing as spare cash for me. I couldn't seem to park cars fast enough or fold shirts neatly enough to rack up a twenty-five-dollar surplus. (By the way, at this point I never used coke to get laid. Girls would ask me if I had it and I'd say, "I wish I did. If you find any let me know." This is against the coke creed. Guys are supposed to lie and say, "Yes, I have some" and then run around and try to buy it. If I actually had some, I was too greedy to fork [spoon] it over. It was a dumb move on my part because the term *coke whore* is no joke. Chicks will do a lot for it. The only thing worse than a coke whore is a coke prude—the girls who snuggle up to you and want to bogart all your stash, and then disappear at the end of the night. There should be a law against all of this. Not that I have experienced either. I have a friend who has.)

Anyway, so I'm at my second job one day, folding clothes. The store was called Johns & Company and was in Phoenix. I was sort of a runner/gofer. I only got the job because I was preppy. (Lame. I get it.) And my brother Andy had worked there forever and had gotten me in. This rich kid came into the store and apparently recognized me from my little bullshit comedy nights. He was sort of freaking out, actually, and it was my first brush with someone acting like I was famous. Even though I was far from it. I was barely local famous, to be honest. He said to me, "I got a new Ferrari out front. It is supercool. You wanna check it out?" "Sure-ly temple!" I replied (trying to live up to my hilarious rep). We went outside and it was a new black 400i. I mumbled the standard car remarks, "Holy shit, this is bitchin', it's cherry, it's tits, etc., etc." He says,

"You want to take a ride??" "Ten-four, good buddy!" (More era-sensitive material. P.S.: It's killing.) We tool around and he asks if I want a bump of the nose candy. After I laugh at the slang term I give him a serious, "Fuck yes." He pulls out his amber vial, but his is fancy. It has a bullet on top, which slides right into the nose and you never have to open the vial. After your first huff, you twist and it reloads for the other side of nose. This was genius! Some Steve Jobs of the dirtball world surely came up with this invention. I was in heaven, AND THEN he told me I could drive the car. All my dreams were coming true. Gacked up on free chalk and driving a Ferrari! If he was a chick it would have been perfect.

Eventually, he dropped me back at Johns & Company and I started cleaning with a renewed sense of purpose and energy. I was really going for the folding merit badge that day. And no one seemed to notice I was amped out of my gourd. Life was good. Coke was better.

So this guy and I started hanging out. Together, we would hit the comedy clubs, I'd do my stupid sets, and he'd hit me with free bumps. We were like Liberace and his sidekick in *Beyond the Candelabra*. Not really, but close. But one day, things took a turn for the shitty. Richie Rich had some good tickets to see Cyndi Lauper, which was a pretty major concert at the time. He had a date that night, so we all went together. The best part of the show (the songs being a distant second) was the unveiling of a new bullet for my schnozz. A TWO-GRAM BULLET, FOLKS! This was like the new iPhone release. I was in awe. All night long I was bumping on his elbow, "Pass it over, Grover." He was so focused on his chick he didn't realize I was double-bumping off it. I did some and then I did some more and I was ready to have fun like all the girls. And then he blindsides me with, "Hey, let's go, I'm going to drop you off, then take her home." I go, "Wait, what??" I couldn't have been more jacked. "I thought we were going to another club." I realized that I needed some booze to even out the gack but he wasn't having it. He wanted to get laid. Too bad for me. (Of course, I do another bump along the way. When in Rome . . . !)

My place was actually my friend's mother's house, even though I'm a big-deal comedian on the Maricopa County comedy circuit. It was about 1 A.M. I creeeeeep up the stairs toward my room. The house is silent. The buzzing in my head is probably the loudest thing in the place. I sprawl out on the bed, but that is no good. Forget about sleeping, there's no way I could even close my eyes at this point. I sneak back downstairs and steal an Old Milwaukee from my pal's stash. My buddy and his parents all have real jobs, and I begin to rationalize my stealing of the beer and my drug buzz by thinking, *I'm in showbiz! I'm different. This is normal!* So I chug down the brew and then head out for a walk, still flying. I feel like I should take a jog over to the Grand Canyon or maybe go dig a pool for my friend. I start getting scared, because I am so energetic. I can't stop. I come back to wake up my friend, thinking I might need to go to the hospital. He looks at me like I am crazy, and then tells me to go lie down and rolls over. This turns out to be the worst advice ever. There I am staring at the ceiling, panting like a dog. It is really disturbing. I wake up my friend again. This time he tells me to breathe into a bag. So I'm going puff . . . puff . . . puff but I don't really understand that I should be breathing out and then breathe in again. I'm totally doing it wrong. Plus, it was a Ziploc bag so it really isn't working. I need to go to a hospital, and that is that.

Now this was a pretty ballsy move, to just show up at the hospital gacked out of my mind. This was right before basketball player Len Bias died of a coke overdose two days after being drafted by the Boston Celtics. If I had known you could actually die from cocaine, I'm pretty sure I would have scared myself into a heart attack.

Once we got to the hospital, I was too scared to go in. I was afraid that the doctors would know I was famous. (I wasn't. I performed at bars during *Monday Night Football* or before karaoke.) So my friend secretly cranked the heat and proceeded to talk me off the ledge for two solid hours. He spent all that time calmly asking me questions to get my mind off the cocaine. Eventually, the sun came up, and I sat there drenched in sweat. "Want to go home?" my friend asks. We head back to his house, and on the way in pass his parents, who are on the way to their jobs. They look at me like I'm a freak, which is more than fair. I spent the day sleeping, like the loser I was.

That wasn't my last run-in with the white dust, but eventually I decide that I'm over it. I can't keep up anymore. Just a little vodka and Diet Coke and I'm good.

ACKNOWLEDGMENTS

Special thanks to Gurvie, Lorne, Venit, Sandler, Caitlin, Levine, Warren, Weitz, Meredith, and my brothers, Andy and Bryan.

Thanks to my assistant Heather and all the folks at Dey Street Books/HarperCollins.

Of course, to Harper.

And to my dad, Sammy. If he hadn't scrammed on us when we were kids I wouldn't be fucked up enough to get a book deal. Thanks Scrammy!

DAVID SPADE is an actor, comedian, and writer. Best known for his dry humor, Spade first hit in the 1990s as a regular cast member and writer on *Saturday Night Live*. After a six-year stint on *SNL*, Spade's career spun off into film, acting alongside energetic funnyman Chris Farley in *Tommy Boy* and *Black Sheep*. Spade was nominated for an Emmy, two Golden Globes, and an American Comedy Award for his role as the wise-cracking, power-hungry assistant on NBC's *Just Shoot Me!* The actor also co-wrote and starred in the cult classic adventure comedy film *Joe Dirt*. Spade reprised his role as the white trash antihero with a stunning mullet in *Joe Dirt 2: Beautiful Loser* in 2015. The comedian lives in Los Angeles, California.